SPIRIT UNTAMED

1994–2025

SPIRIT UNTAMED

1994–2025

AJAZ AHMED

HENI PUBLISHING, LONDON

First published in 2025

Copyright © Ajaz Ahmed

A catalogue record for this book is available from the British Library.

ISBN: 978-1-911736-30-1

2 4 6 8 10 9 7 5 3 1

Edited by Peter Lyle
Design and typography by Phil Beresford
Cover and illustrations by Johnny Budden

Publisher: HENI Publishing, London, United Kingdom

EU Authorised Representative: Easy Access System Europe –
Mustamäe tee 50, 10621 Tallinn, Estonia, gpsr.requests@easproject.com

FSC
www.fsc.org
MIX
Paper | Supporting
responsible forestry
FSC® C114687

To Tom Bedecarré,
who believed in the dream
and in me

To my mother, Sughran,
whose grace and compassion
set my spirit free

To Aaron + Isaac,
They tell you that you will love your kids.
What they don't tell you is that you
will fall in love with them. Dada

Ajaz Ahmed founded AKQA at the age of 21. From a small start-up, the company grew to employ over 5,000 people across five continents, winning an unprecedented 81 Agency of the Year awards along the way. *Spirit Untamed* is his fourth book, following *Velocity*, *Limitless*, and *Defeat*. In 2025, Ajaz co-founded Studio.One, a new company to explore what's possible when human imagination and adaptive intelligence work in harmony.

CONTENTS

I

The Entrepreneurial Spirit

2

When Creativity Meets Technology

3

Beyond Business

4

Origins & Inspirations

5
Brands & Values

6
Dreams & Discipline

A TIME OF QUIET
BETWEEN THE STORMS

Thirty years is a long time to be doing one job.

On 16 October 2024, with a fountain pen my late father left me, I signed the final separation papers from AKQA, the company I founded, helped to build and led for three decades. The date felt significant. It was exactly eight years to the day since my father passed away. I figured I would grieve both losses on the same day – my father's absence and the closing of a chapter that had defined much of my adult life.

When you give so much of yourself to a cause, it doesn't stop when you step away. It stays with you – in the questions unanswered and in business unfinished.

A few days after I resigned, a client called. He suggested that 30 years in one role is not something you see every day and that I should celebrate the achievements of those years – gather friends, colleagues and clients, and mark the occasion. He believed that a proper send-off would help put the past to bed. But understandably, I wasn't in the mood for a party.

Still, the client was right about the importance of resolving the loose ends. This book is, in many ways, my attempt at hemming the frayed edges into something whole. It's a collection of thoughts and reflections gathered along the way. It's a way of processing, understanding, and, ultimately, letting go.

This collection isn't a conclusion. It's a celebration of what's been as prologue to what's next.

The future isn't just another chapter.

It's a whole new story.

I

The Entrepreneurial Spirit

*How ideas, dedication and
optimism build better businesses*

Don't fight over a bigger slice. Bake a better pie

Why zero-sum thinking stifles growth

GROWTH: A UNIVERSAL ASPIRATION GONE AWRY

'Growth' has long been a fundamental business aspiration. It's as natural and ancient an ambition for the person who starts a business as it is for the farmer who wants their crops to thrive or the parent who wants to nurture a child to a fulfilling adulthood.

But since 2008, growth has become such a singular and short-term preoccupation that, in many cases, it begins to look like a self-sabotaging one. Bad businesses relentlessly downgrade products, increase prices and then wonder where the customer loyalty and assets they shed in the name of 'efficiency' have gone. National governments have increasingly spoken of 'growth' as their ultimate objective – but singularly failed to sell this idea to their citizens. They talk about the need to 'compete' with the economies of countries with much bigger populations, lower wages and larger manufacturing bases. They justify cuts to services and long-term investments as necessary sacrifices along the way.

No wonder that voters, seeing no improvement in their daily lives while the world's wealthy get wealthier, are increasingly attracted to politicians whose rhetoric is less about growing the existing system and more about torching it.

THE PIE CHART MENTALITY: A RECIPE FOR DIVISION

What do bad corporate managers and unpopular politicians have in common? When politicians make cuts, they invariably fall back on metaphors that make economists roll their eyes: the weekly household budget, the maxed-out credit card. When managers diminish their products or services in the name of greater gains, it seems to me they're stuck with an even more antiquated and simplistic visual metaphor. A metaphor deeply ingrained in our minds from our school days, or the first corporate reports we ever read as impressionable teens: the pie chart.

There is one pie on the table, and the name of the game is the same as it was when you were a greedy kid: How do I make sure I get the biggest slice?

Corporate managers often operate within a zero-sum framework in which resources, power and opportunities are perceived as finite. According to this mindset, one person's gain is another's loss – a psychology which, in turn, fosters an environment of competition that can lead to exclusion and division among teams and individuals. This perspective frequently forces managers to pick sides, creating winners and losers within an organisation and leaving some employees or departments feeling undervalued or marginalised.

WHEN BUSINESS BECAME WAR: MACHIAVELLI, SUN TZU AND THEIR BUSINESS SCHOOL 'SOLDIERS'

Outside the walls of the organisation, the effects of this mindset are equally attritional. The inevitable outcome of the zero-sum mentality is a tendency to see going into business as the same as going into battle: a quest to secure the biggest portion of contested territory and resources, with your very survival at stake.

In the 1990s, influenced as much by the image of *Wall Street*, the movie (the one from the man who wrote *Scarface* and framed both stories of two sides of one coin) as Wall Street, the New York address, the idea of business as war really boomed in management circles. 'Machiavellian' went from being a slur to an ideal. Ancient tomes such as *The Art of War* became the latest things to quote.

But the boardroom generals who signed up to this ideology overlooked some important things. Niccolò Machiavelli was undoubtedly an intelligent and observant diplomat and thinker. But he operated in a time when his home state, Florence, was in a perpetual state of actual war, with powerful families jostling over control. His insights in *The Prince* didn't come from meritocracies – that is, from the kind of system good businesses and true democracies should be – but from observing the operations of royalty and nobility: the arbitrary, hereditary rule of the richest and most powerful families in a territory. The success of his theories in the real world was partial and fleeting. It was only when he retired from public life that he found true fulfilment in writing, whether his treatises on such subjects as leadership or his theatrical plays.

Sun Tzu's *Art of War* was another touchstone for the kind of manager who weaponised the notion of business as a zero-sum game. But it's just as easy to find warnings from the great Chinese general of the perils of seeing business as war, as it is to find encouragement to think that way. "All warfare is based on deception," Sun Tzu wrote. If you see business as war, you spend all your time trying to outwit and deceive the competition instead of focusing on improving your own offer.

POISONOUS OFFICE POLITICS: THE COLLATERAL DAMAGE OF THE ZERO-SUM SENSIBILITY

In zero-sum management structures, this conflict-centred philosophy is rarely restricted to the competition. Once you champion the idea that business is war, it's very difficult not to bring the war back home to your organisation. In the famous words of another celebrated military strategist, Prussian general Carl von Clausewitz, "War is the continuation of politics by other means". We've all known people who get ahead by focusing all their energy on office politics and treating their own organisation as a kind of conflict zone. But once this ideology is embedded in a corporate culture, it necessarily means that time, energy and creativity that should be concentrated on improving your offering to consumers or shareholders is instead expended on making gains at the expense of your colleagues. It means you're wasting salaries, pensions and desk space on people who aren't allowed to contribute and whose only role is to become cannon fodder for scheming colleagues.

Every minute spent strategising about how to get ahead at the expense of workmates is a minute not spent on improving your offering to customers or innovation. Every day consumed by the machinations of your office is a day when you could have been out talking to people, observing their behaviour, listening to them, or otherwise finding inspiration for a new and better way of doing things.

THE ENTREPRENEURIAL MINDSET: ABUNDANCE OVER SCARCITY

True entrepreneurs, on the other hand, tend to adopt a mindset of abundance. They don't fight over the size of their slice of the pie. They just bake a new pie. Maybe even lots of pies. They are driven by the belief that value can be created, often from scratch, through innovation and resourcefulness. Entrepreneurs maximise the utility of available assets and seek opportunities where others see only limitations. They make golden businesses out of base material others think worthless. There's an inspirational, alchemical allure to the practice of real entrepreneurs. It's a kind of magic that governments, too, should channel if they really want to get their electorates on board with their growth agendas.

A SYMPHONY OF GROWTH: LESSONS FROM THE ORIGINS OF ENTREPRENEURSHIP

Evidence of these truths can be located in the origins of the word 'entrepreneur' itself. The very first individuals to be labelled entrepreneurs were Parisian businesspeople who took the rarefied world of classical chamber music, then the privilege of wealthy aristocrats, to large halls on a scale that greatly increased access and trusted that the public would have the ability to appreciate it. This development led to a host of innovations, from new instruments like the modern piano to the development of the orchestra and the symphony, the continent-wide celebrity of composers including Beethoven and Mozart and the 'golden age' of classical music to which they were central.

The genuinely entrepreneurial mindset encourages collaboration and inclusivity, as growth and success are not viewed as finite but as virtues that can expand through creativity, vision and effort. In this way, entrepreneurs build cultures that thrive on shared potential rather than competition for scarce resources. Why reduce good business to a squabble for a bigger slice for yourself when it could be an opportunity to put something better on everybody's plate?

Losing a job isn't the end. It can be a new beginning

Being 'let go' is horrible. But being set free can be the greatest gift of all. There's no such thing as a good time to lose your job. But this year's firing season seems especially long and cruel. Just when you think you're safe, you discover the last round of job cuts is simply the warm-up. Just as you're thanking your lucky stars that your employer hasn't opted for the industry-standard six per cent, you find out that they've decided to trump the competition and wow the markets with an audacious ten.

It's all too easy for redundancy to knock a person's faith. The abrupt loss of an environment where colleagues and management acknowledge your contribution and value can quickly see doubt gnaw away at even the most assured. A generosity of spirit, faith in teamwork, and a sense that good work gets rewarded: these can soon seem like unaffordable luxuries.

That's why a profound and heartfelt gesture like Cameron Rout's goes beyond any measure. It started with a humble LinkedIn post Rout made after being let go from Google: "GOOGLE LAYOFF START-UP", began the text, "Who's in? Hit me up right now, I want to chat with everyone. (not just xooglers!)." He went on to succinctly remind people that the tens of thousands released by tech giants are a highly skilled cohort who, at a moment when investors are eager for new start-ups to back, could pool their considerable talents and make something new, instead of fighting one another over any oversubscribed new openings at established organisations.

On the first day, 1.5 million people read the post, and 2,000 wrote to express interest in joining him. Now, a couple of months later, more than 25 new start-ups are in the works, thanks to his wise gesture.

Something similar happened in 2002 when the collapses of Enron and WorldCom led to the demise of their auditor Arthur Andersen. That company was named after the man who founded it in the early 20th century. For decades, it grew by adhering to his founding values of stewardship, professionalism and the refusal to let the need to retain clients compromise the core mission of transparency for investors and regulators. By the end, these values had been corrupted and cast aside.

Tens of thousands who lost their jobs in the fallout swiftly came together to start successful new accounting and auditing businesses which remain significant players in the market today. A brand is just a name when it forgets what it stands for, but a person's talent, skills and capacity to contribute don't disappear when their job title is taken away.

Let's be clear: however great or small the loss, no well-intentioned words can fill the gap it leaves. But let's not forget another simple truth: you can't discover something new about yourself or realise your true potential without the risk of getting lost to explore a different direction.

Being 'let go' is horrible. But being set free can be a detour to a better destination.

— First published April 2023 —

Why so many of the world's best chief executives are Indian

One in six of the Fortune 500 tech companies are run by people of Indian heritage. From family values to education and entrepreneurial spirit, India offers lessons from which Britain could learn.

With its duration of 44 days and 970 million registered voters, India's epic and gigantic general election is finally winding up. In the global business world, though, the question of Indian leadership already appears to have been decided.

Indian-born chief executives now lead many of the world's most valuable companies. Shares in Google, Microsoft and IBM – led by Sundar Pichai, Satya Nadella and Arvind Krishna, respectively – are trading at, or near, all-time highs. One in six of the 60 tech companies on the Fortune 500 list of the biggest US companies are run by people of Indian heritage.

And it's by no means a tech sector thing: defying the luxury slowdown, Chanel recently reported record revenue of $20 billion (£16 billion) last year, up 16 per cent compared to 2022. Its chief executive, Leena Nair, is also Indian-born, while Indra Nooyi ran PepsiCo for 12 years, propelling the career of Laxman Narasimhan, who went on to run Dettol giant Reckitt Benckiser in the UK before heading to the US to lead Starbucks.

Although the latest published data confirms India's position as the world's fastest-growing economy among the G20 nations, the country's booming export trade in chief executives feels like the bigger story.

That said, we don't hear much about it – which is understandable. Rightly wary of bracketing people according to old-fashioned notions of 'national character', diversity-aware businesspeople worry how they'd phrase the questions. Key witnesses are also good at not engaging with it. Doing interviews to accompany the launch of his autobiography a couple of years ago, Nadella would skilfully reveal how his success had been shaped by his home life and the greater forces of world history. But when asked about what made Indians so successful in modern business, he would gracefully reroute his answer, preferring to talk about other famous alumni of his Hyderabad Public School or the virtues of migrant workers at large.

I understand the impulse to avoid direct answers to such questions as "What's the secret?" or "Explain the 'Indian Way'". But I also understand the desire to ask. After all, it's instinctive to seek insights that improve business. As an entrepreneur with Indian ancestry who increasingly finds these questions put to him, I've come up with some answers. Roughly half are about a broad-brush understanding of Indian culture and education, but the rest are about India's sheer vastness and variety.

A CULTURE OF LEARNING

A positive attitude towards learning and ambition often begins in the home, where knowledge is prized in Indian culture. The last available figures for national average reading time spent per week had India in the lead (at more than ten hours), whereas the UK and the US didn't even make the top 20. My own Indian-born father had little interest in commerce, but when I handed him a copy of my first published book, it put a glint in his eye. (His suggestion that I read the dictionary as a child had finally paid off.)

Reflecting on how Indian-Americans dominate spelling contests in the US despite comprising only one per cent of its population, the author Nikhil Raval emphasised the importance of time spent with family, instilling the eloquence, confidence and tenacity to excel.

FAMILY VALUES

In Indian business, 'family' is not only the picture on your phone's home screen of the smiling cherubs you haven't seen all week but also a fundamental framework for structuring business and rewarding employees. Although the West may think of building empires, Eastern counterparts tend to focus on creating dynasties.

Indian workers are more likely to have grown up in the kind of intergenerational environments that have become rare in other economies in recent decades and to have witnessed plenty of poverty and need in their daily lives. Rather than fire, rehire and constantly restructure in the name of a grand business strategy, Indian firms are better at providing training and delegating decision-making.

A sense of loyalty is fostered not through financial incentives alone but by encouraging initiative, nurturing ambition and frequently acknowledging someone's contribution to a firm's greater goals – which, more often than not, have a significant societal aspect.

GREAT UNIVERSITIES

At school, rigorous maths and English drills are still an elemental part of education, and education itself is still regarded as a route to finding yourself the employment you desire – rather than a journey of self-discovery to 'find yourself'. Well-funded and elite students can attend Indian Institutes of Technology, which were modelled on the Massachusetts Institute of Technology's ethos, interdisciplinary approach and collaborations with business. Dubbed 'production lines for CEOs', their origins go back to 1950, when India established a network of engineering and technology institutes three years after achieving independence.

FLEXIBILITY

Not everyone has access to a good education, which brings us to perhaps the greatest asset of Indian business – one less about culture and more about catering for every strata of Indian society. One fascinating *Harvard Business Review* report focuses on a specific line of work – Mumbai's lunch-delivery network. It explains how the city's *dabbawalas* use its most dependable transport systems (rail and bicycle) to get the right lunchboxes to hundreds of thousands of workers punctually and with uncanny accuracy. Based on a colour-coded system dating back to the 19th century, it means even those lacking literacy can get work and are rewarded for their entrepreneurial instincts.

The dabbawalas are just one of many examples of how Indian business know-how seems to be less about a singular culture or set of rules and more about a flexible and holistic approach that naturally equips leaders to adapt as they steer companies with operations across the globe. Indian-origin leaders of multinationals have already engaged with a national population whose experience spans every extreme of wealth and poverty, massively varying levels of education and modern and traditional methods of doing things. More important than adhering to a rigid blueprint crafted in the confines of the boardroom is navigating a path to prosperity by finding common ground and shared connections across an incredibly diverse range of people and places.

IMMIGRANT ENTREPRENEURIALISM

More than 20 million Indians live abroad, making them the world's largest diaspora. The immigrant experience and entrepreneurship have always gone hand in hand. Read interviews with Bridgewater Associates' Italian-American Ray Dalio or Nvidia's Taiwanese-born Jensen Huang, and you will find they cite the same experiences as those who went before them. Growing up multicultural and multilingual makes for an agile mind and an innate ability to see there is more than one way of looking at the world. Not feeling like you fit in means you are wary of the kind of complacency that will see you suspected of stereotypical failings. Being different at school often compels you to build inner resilience and locks you out of the peer-group cliques that sidetrack so many promising people from pursuing their youthful passions into working life.

LESSONS FOR BRITAIN

Whatever its issues and inequalities, America's self-image remains that of a nation of immigrants where anybody can make it to the top. In the UK, though, we've become accustomed to talking about jobs that 'British people won't do' – skilled roles in farming or the care sector that we know are essential to modern life but in which opportunities for good pay or self-advancement are scarce. If we want to cultivate better leadership, perhaps a practical first step would be for the next government to think about the virtues of creating more opportunities and support so that even those on the lower rung get their chance to excel, too.

— First published in The Sunday Times *in June 2024 —*

Entrepreneurs need to have creativity, courage, responsiveness and resilience

ALL ASPIRING ENTREPRENEURS SHOULD
READ RUDYARD KIPLING'S 'IF' — EVERY WORD
OF ADVICE IN IT IS FOR THE AGES.

"If you can keep your head when all around you are losing theirs …" Rudyard Kipling's 'If' is often voted the UK's favourite poem. As an aspiring entrepreneur preparing for the adventure ahead, you could do worse than read it or reread it. Its elegant third verse may have even been written for entrepreneurs. But every bit of its advice – lead, but don't stop listening; be willing to bet it all and start again without resentment; don't let success or failure go to your head; go with what's right, not what's easy – is for the ages. It's especially relevant for times like the present, when the global economy and wider culture are transforming in all sorts of dramatic ways.

New ideas and inventions that influence culture, affect society and contribute to the pool of human progress will continue to come our way fast. If anything, they will accelerate exponentially, as shown by the most innovative organisations and start-ups using the newest technology to create the next technology.

The UK has been described as a nation of shopkeepers. I'm not so sure about that label, but it may always be a nation of eccentrics. The history of British innovation is packed with scientists, inventors, artists and entrepreneurs whose outsider perspectives were crucial to their eventual achievement. By refusing to accept conventional ways of looking at things, they saw opportunities and discoveries in areas that most people were blind to. By pursuing odd hobbies and unlikely obsessions, they opened up incredible new vistas to everybody.

If you asked me for a contemporary UK inspiration for entrepreneurs, I wouldn't choose a business, but rather the Nobel Prize-winning physicists at Manchester University working on graphene, the carbon-derived super-substance. Incredibly strong and flexible, graphene has dozens of potential applications, from medicine to energy saving.

MAKE IT HAPPEN

It's an entrepreneur's mission to make things happen – to make the worthy worthwhile; to make what could be bland irresistibly sexy; make what might be obscured impossible to ignore. These are the kinds of challenges that have inspired entrepreneurs to invent industries, transform economies, create careers (where others saw dead ends) and upturn archaic thinking.

Of course, sometimes, their schemes don't come off – whether because of their own failings or because they are doomed by wider circumstances. Because you're venturing into new territory, you have to be at peace with the idea that once you've given a venture your all, unknown external and future factors could still scupper it. That's why rigour and resilience are absolutely crucial. If your organisation is lean, street-wise, agile and adaptive, you can recover and stay the course after those setbacks.

The most admired entrepreneurs counterbalance creativity and experimentation with organisational eminence and responsive systems. As a teenager, about the same time that I started reading public company annual reports, I also got into sailing. The secrets of the two didn't seem so different to me and still don't. Hurtling into a high-stakes, untested but meticulously well-planned project as part of a well-engineered company is never plain sailing. It's more like the thrill of sailing at full pelt downwind, but knowing your mast won't break, nor your boat capsize because all the correct physical structures, engineering and navigational tools are in place. When you seek unexplored terrain and push the limits, sometimes the limits push back.

If you've got the resilience and rigour, you probably have boldness and belief too. Entrepreneurs aren't ashamed to use the word 'vision' because that is, by definition, their most important quality: the ability to live in the world as it is, yet to see it as it could be. In the words of Kipling: *"If you can fill the unforgiving minute, with sixty seconds' worth of distance run, yours is the Earth and everything that's in it."*

— Originally published in The Guardian *in February 2013 —*

The class ceiling

How did entrepreneurialism become a playground of the wealthy? And how can it get back to its egalitarian roots?

SELECTIVE ACCESS AND STUNTED GROWTH

Here's an incredibly simple and obvious truth: if you conduct a talent search, but you only permit five per cent of people to enter, you're going to miss out on a lot of talent. Or, to put it another way: if your economic goal is growth, but you consign the vast majority of potential wealth-creators to a fate as undervalued wage slaves, your ideas don't add up. It doesn't take a mathematical genius to see that. Yet today we find ourselves in a culture where economic and business leaders talk constantly about the need for growth and champion social mobility, yet fail to take the steps to enable it. Entrepreneurialism – the means by which all people have gotten ahead in life since the first farmers and traders – has become the preserve of the wealthy.

ENTREPRENEURIALISM: THE OUTSIDER'S WAY IN

Like many people who grew up to be entrepreneurs, I was not what most people think of as a normal kid. Instead of comics or pop music magazines, I grew up reading biographies and memoirs of entrepreneurs. As a child of parents who had grown up in another country, culture and language – parents who worked hard jobs for long hours to provide the basics for their kids – I developed confidence and conviction from what I learned in them. I learned that it didn't matter that I was not rich, connected, heir to a business empire, or to the British manner born – indeed, I learned that if I wanted to make my own way in business, those things could actually be assets.

Think of Ray Dalio, the $14 billion hedge fund manager born to Italian parents in New York, who didn't fit in at school and got his first breaks caddying at the local golf course. Consider Jensen Huang, who has led Nvidia to its current market-dominating status, and who as a child was sent from Taiwan to the US, where he faced prejudice and privations but found ways too reach out to his schoolmates. If the USA is the global home of entrepreneurialism, perhaps that's also because it's also a nation of immigrants. In a new place where you aren't always made to feel welcome or can be confused by unfamiliar customs, money and the making of money can become the *lingua franca* of success and belonging.

When I dropped out of higher education to start a business, I could – and did – look to another outsider who did it his way: Steve Jobs, who left his degree course at Reed College to pursue his own path, yet would later end up giving new Stanford graduates an inspirational speech that has gone down in history; was motivated by a questing, restless spirit; and was ultimately one of the most influential business voices of our time.

Drifters and dropouts found success, and so did lots of groups who diverged from the norm. A comprehensive academic survey of entrepreneurs' backgrounds published a few years ago tracked how many other kinds of outsiders found their 'in' through self-made business success: people who were differently abled and people who had suffered exclusion, losses and struggles that made them resilient and forced them to find their own way.

Locked out from the mainstream, from existing networks of power and influence and established paths to success, outsiders are compelled to observe, innovate and escape received wisdom just to survive. William Blake's famous declaration of his artistic soul always seemed to me to resonate with the essence of true entrepreneurialism: "I must create my own system or be enslaved by another man's. I will not reason and compare: my business is to create."

As a young person coming of age in a United Kingdom where class barriers and clubby networks were much more overt than they appear today, I also understood entrepreneurs as people who smashed through these categories. For every success story of a post-1960s middle-class kid who'd started a boutique, Thatcher's Britain had scores of what snobs disparagingly called 'barrow boys' – working-class people who moved from the world of running market stalls to making a mint as stock market traders.

WHERE DID OUR GET-UP-AND-GO GO?

Because entrepreneurs invent new products, markets and services and so often thrive outside the status quo, or even define themselves against it, we might reflexively assume that the entrepreneurial spirit is immune to the greater forces that impact upon other employment opportunities. We're used to reading about how jobs in acting, music and the arts are increasingly preserves of the children of wealthy parents and how people newly graduated in high-status skills such as law struggle now to land and afford the internships they need to complete their qualifications. The fact that entrepreneurship is suffering the same way doesn't make as many headlines. But it should – especially considering the economic impact of all the potential currently being wasted.

Numerous factors feed the decline in entrepreneurialism impacting the UK – and many other leading economies around the world – today. That time-honoured route from market stall to stock market, or local greengrocer to global supermarket chain, has been affected by the wider travails of physical retail. That Saturday job in a local shop, once a springboard that enabled you to save for your own plans and get an understanding of customer needs, is a thing of the past. Outside of a few sectors, apprenticeships have also become more elusive and less useful, discarded or downgraded by the quick-fix mentality of some businesses. Successive governments have promoted academic over vocational training, nominally aiming to enable social mobility and access for all but in practice often saddling young people with near-useless qualifications and massive debts.

And talking of debts, we have to acknowledge how the current economic climate negatively impacts ambition and opportunity. A recent survey by the UK homelessness charity Shelter found that two thirds of households in work now struggle to make monthly rental payments. Millions of working families depend on state benefits to keep their families going. We know that most new businesses fail and that success is frequently built on the lessons of experiments that don't work out. When people feel that trying to better their circumstances puts them at risk of losing everything, they lose the impetus to do something new.

REBUILDING THE LADDER

There's no silver bullet for tackling the deep-seated structural problems that face would-be working-class entrepreneurs in today's economy. But there are practical measures governments could take to improve access and expand the pool of potential successes. They can reinvigorate training and education to equip aspiring talent with the tools to make it in the marketplace.

Businesses, too, can do better at providing networks of expertise and mentorship to people starting out in business. If wealthy people can get out of the hoarding mindset and start sharing their know-how and connections, we'll all benefit. A can-do attitude is inspiring and contagious, and if the entrepreneurial talent for finding value where others don't is distributed to a greater chunk of the populace, the entire economy stands to gain. If you are crossing fingers for, let alone betting on, a prosperous future, why sabotage the odds of it happening by locking so many people out from making a contribution? Until the mass of people feel empowered to harness their imaginations and pursue their deepest aspirations, we'll remain in a cycle of class immobility and cultural stagnation.

Entrepreneurship schools could inspire the next generation of leaders

At the age of 12, despite a relatively good academic performance, I was told by my school careers adviser to follow in my father's footsteps to become a factory worker rather than attempt to overstep social barriers.

Fortunately, I grew up in an era that had household names such as Richard Branson, Anita Roddick, Paul Smith and the Saatchi brothers. I saw them on television, read about them in Sunday supplements, and even requested their company reports, which I pored over with the enthusiasm many kids reserved for favourite record sleeves or Panini sticker collections.

Without this alternative education on how to get ahead in life and business, I might not have been emboldened to ignore the then-standard state school advice to stay in my lane.

What these entrepreneurs taught me was the alchemical power of ambition. Not to be confused with greed, self-aggrandisement or the steamrollering of other people's desires in pursuit of your own, the kind of ambition those household names embodied seemed to be an entirely beneficial thing. It had the power to change your life, enrich the lives of employees, make a positive difference to society and even evoke national pride.

The quality that made me look on these famous names as people I could legitimately view as inspiration was how distinctly British they made ambition seem. Ambition was the secret ingredient for combining the great British virtues of eccentricity and enterprise. It also extended to engineering, where pioneers such as James Dyson were celebrated by taking that tradition into the electronic age. Ambition was as British as apple crumble.

Thirty years ago, inspired by such stories and by my faith in emerging technologies, I founded the digital innovation agency AKQA. In the beginning, evangelising the importance of the internet was a tough sell. Many companies initially viewed it as either a gimmick or an afterthought, but we got enough business from big brands to gain a foothold.

Over time, despite the dotcom crash, the global banking meltdown, and the long, dark nights when all seemed doomed, we kept believing and were well positioned when most companies came to appreciate the importance of this new arena. We now have 5,500 employees in 50 studios across 30 countries.

In Britain, growth stories like AKQA's are scarce. Despite shows like *The Apprentice* and *Dragons' Den* streaming on our screens and our social media feeds being full of future moguls, the UK seems to be losing its connection to the start-up and scale-up spirit.

When the existing system is failing too many people and business plans, a culture of ambition – and the courage and imagination required to realise it – is a vital force for turning around those structural problems. Rising living and borrowing costs, softer consumer demand and post-Brexit complications undoubtedly contribute to this ambition deficit. If I had the ear of the government or the opposition, I'd argue more for the value of nurturing networks of support, mentorships and belief.

Pessimism leads to a sense of powerlessness and resignation. Ambition serves as an antidote, igniting the drive to overcome obstacles. The celebrated anthropologist Wade Davis says: "The most important thing is to recognise that pessimism is an indulgence, orthodoxy is the enemy of invention and despair is an insult to the imagination. You have to do what needs to be done and only then ask whether it was possible or permissible."

A deficiency in digital skills costs the British economy £63 billion a year in lost GDP. Chronic underinvestment and limited access to long-term capital have resulted in UK productivity trailing behind the US, Germany and France. This week's budget maintained a stable framework but lacked transformative measures or anything to motivate risk-averse youth.

Addressing Britain's entrenched regional inequalities and their detrimental impact necessitates political consensus and shielding long-term structural policies from the volatility of electoral cycles.

Little more than a decade ago, Ben Francis, the founder of sportswear manufacturer and retailer Gymshark, had the ambition to create a British contender to Adidas and Nike. His aspiration catapulted Solihull-headquartered Gymshark's value beyond £1 billion.

When Ben was at school, entrepreneurship wasn't a subject in the curriculum. It should be now. Introducing a GCSE and A-level in entrepreneurship, alongside the launch of dedicated regional 'schools of entrepreneurship', could empower individuals with the guidance, communal support and financial backing required to pursue new ventures effectively.

"Human beings are not created as job seekers," the Nobel Prize laureate and social business pioneer Professor Muhammad Yunus said. "They are born as entrepreneurs."

Instead of merely guiding youth to choose from the well-trodden path of existing options, perhaps careers advisers should inspire a new generation to blaze their own trails and build the big companies of tomorrow. There's no shortage of challenges waiting to be transformed into visionary opportunities.

— First published in The Sunday Times *in March 2024 —*

The harvest and the hustle

Three types of managers in the corporate field

BUSINESS AS FARM: THE THREE SCHOOLS OF MANAGEMENT

In a broad-brush sense, managing a business is like running a farm. Specifically, the work of arable farming, where crops and produce are planted and harvested and where the latest technologies coexist with time-honoured annual customs (think of the harvest in the autumn or the new financial year in the spring).

Both of these roles require vision, patience and a deep understanding of cycles – knowing when to repeat the cycle of planting, when to harvest and when to innovate. In the business world, the 'field' is the company or organisation, and the managers are the farmers entrusted with its care. But not all managers approach this responsibility in the same way. Just as different farming techniques can either nurture or deplete the long-term fertility of the soil, different management styles either sustain or undermine a business over time.

Whether they realise it or not, every decision a manager makes is like planting a seed in the soil of their organisation. Some seeds take root, sprout and grow into flourishing plants. Others wither away, unable to survive in the toxic or depleted ground in which they were planted. In business, as in farming, the quality of the soil determines the outcome.

This is my conceptual framework for working out what type of person is managing your 'farm' at any given time, what type of manager you actually need and what kind of results you can expect in the next year's harvest – and the years to come – with each one allowing the old to make way for the new.

Each of these three kinds of managers – the 'farmers', the 'caretakers' or the 'reapers' – plays a role, for better or worse, in the life cycle of a business. The farmers are the ones who plant new seeds, nurturing ideas and people with a long-term vision in mind. The reapers are the ones who, through relentless restructuring and short-term tactics, strip the soil of its nutrients, cashing in quickly but eroding the foundation of what already exists in the process. And then there are the caretakers, those who tend to the status quo, maintaining what has been built – but with little innovation and insufficient adaptation to changes in the environment and the market, ensuring that over time the crop will inevitably decline.

THE FARMER: PLANTING SEEDS FOR TOMORROW

The farmer is the manager who plants new seeds. They see potential where others see only the landscape in front of them. For farmers, every project, every product and every person is fertile ground for growth. They invest in people, ideas and processes that might not yield immediate results, but will bear fruit in the seasons to come. Farmers understand that to create sustainable value, you must think beyond the next quarter's earnings report.

In the modern business environment, it's easy to overlook the importance of long-term thinking. Shareholders demand instant results, and the pace of change is relentless. But farmers know that some of the most valuable innovations – the ones that will keep the company relevant in the next decade and beyond – require patience. They invest in research and development, build the skills of their teams and foster a culture of curiosity and experimentation. Farmers aren't afraid of failure because they understand that growth is a process. A failed experiment is just another form of learning that generates a new lesson to be taken into the next season.

This type of manager is increasingly rare, but their influence is profound. Companies that thrive over the long term often owe their success to farmers who, at some point, sowed the seeds of future innovation and ensured that the business not only survived but also grew in new and unexpected ways. Farmers know that every great success begins with planting a seed.

THE REAPER: HARVESTING WITHOUT PLANTING

The second type of manager is the 'reaper', the one bent on maximising yields at all costs. These are the leaders who come in and shake things up, often taking pride in being agents of 'change'. But more often than not, their idea of change proves destructive rather than constructive. They slash costs, initiate frequent restructures and make decisions based on short-term financial metrics rather than long-term value creation.

At first glance, these managers may seem effective. After all, their actions often result in immediate improvements to the bottom line. Cutting staff, selling off assets and reducing investments can all make a balance sheet look healthier – for a while. But over time, the true cost of this approach becomes apparent.

Reapers are often hailed as turnaround experts and might even be seen as necessary – flagging firms often turn to such figures in tough times. We've certainly seen a large number of them of late, but in reality, they are robbing the future to pay for the present. Their relentless pursuit of short-term gains at the expense of long-term stability weakens the very foundations they are supposed to be strengthening.

Interviewed during his absence from Apple in the 1990s, Steve Jobs argued that the management team that had succeeded him at the firm enjoyed several years of great financial results but then abruptly sunk into crisis because its singular focus on quick profit meant it had failed to expand market share or nurture customer loyalty, which had led to sudden irrelevance.

By that stage, Jobs complained, Apple's management had already 'won' by allocating themselves outsized and unnecessary personal rewards instead of investing in the experience of the end user. This brings us to another dimension of the reaper's impact. Used to being rushed in as a quick fix before moving on, such leaders naturally incline towards certain habits, like maximising personal rewards while in the role or parachuting in their own loyalists rather than going through the time-consuming and conscientious process of carefully appraising the talent the company already has. This leads to the kind of self-serving and tactical decisions which erode a company's resources, culture and reputation. Instead of fostering innovation or product design, they focus on consolidating their own influence. Without a courageous and experienced board of directors, they weaken an organisation and demoralise its workforce.

Innovation stalls, talent leaves and the organisation begins to hollow out from within. The soil that once supported growth becomes barren, and the business begins to wither. In farming, over-harvesting leads to exhausted soil. In business, over-exploiting resources – people, products or brand equity – without tending the land and nurturing new growth leads to decline. Reapers leave behind a landscape of diminished potential – one that, even if it doesn't mark the beginning of the end of a business, will leave it in straits that will take years, if not decades, to recover from.

Then there are the caretakers, the managers who maintain the status quo. They aren't planting new seeds, but they aren't destroying value either. Instead, they maintain the systems, processes and products that have worked in the past. Caretakers keep the business running without necessarily driving it forward.

Caretakers often emerge during periods of stability. The company has had a successful run, and the main goal is to keep things steady. There's nothing inherently wrong with this approach, but it carries an inherent risk: businesses that stand still in a fast-moving world eventually fall behind. Just as a farm that keeps producing the same crops each season, regardless of changing consumer tastes and commodity prices, slowly fades until it becomes unprofitable or ripe for a predatory buyout by a bigger agricultural conglomerate, so businesses that rely solely on what worked yesterday will see diminishing returns over time.

Caretakers can sustain a business for a time, but without new perspectives or innovations, decline is inevitable. Maintenance alone rarely breeds renewed success. In an age where disruption is constant and consumer expectations are always evolving, simply carrying on as before is a dangerous game. The crops will still grow, but eventually the yields will be smaller, and the land will become less fertile.

THE BALANCE

In a healthy business ecosystem, all three types of managers might coexist, but it's the farmer who ultimately drives progress. Reapers should be kept on a short leash, only called upon in extreme circumstances and monitored to ensure they don't strip the business of its potential. Caretakers can be valuable, especially during times of stability, but they must also be ready to embrace change when the time comes.

The challenge for any organisation is to recognise the type of managers they have in place and ensure the right balance is struck. A company dominated by reapers (value destroyers) might show impressive short-term gains, but it will eventually collapse under its own weight. An organisation filled with caretakers will run smoothly for a time, but it will gradually dwindle into irrelevance. And although a company led by farmers will likely experience growing pains and harvests where foresight and patience eat into immediate profits, it will also be the one most likely to thrive in the long term.

Business, like farming, is a delicate balance between planting, maintaining and harvesting. The managers who understand this will be the ones who ensure their companies are not only profitable today but also sustainable tomorrow. Whether we are planting new ideas, maintaining what already works or restructuring for the future, it is essential to know that each season demands a different approach. Just as in farming, the richest fields are those that have been carefully tended, nurtured and renewed. In business, the same principles apply. Only those who plant the seeds today will reap the rewards tomorrow.

A FERTILE BUSINESS: CULTURE,
INNOVATION AND TRUST

It's up to us – the farmers of the corporate field – to cultivate environments where ideas, people and growth can thrive. A fertile business environment is one where ideas are planted, nurtured and given the opportunity to grow. But how do we cultivate such soil?

It starts with culture. Culture is the foundation of every business, the soil from which everything else grows. Just as a farmer tends to the earth to ensure it's rich with nutrients, decision-makers in business must nurture their company culture to ensure it supports creativity, innovation and trust. A toxic culture, on the other hand, is like barren soil – nothing can grow in it. No matter how talented the employees or how brilliant the ideas, they won't thrive in an environment that stifles collaboration and mishandles delegation. New approaches won't develop in a culture that discourages risk-taking or breeds mistrust.

Next is innovation, because culture alone is not enough. The soil must be enriched with the willingness to embrace change, experiment with new approaches and seek better ways of doing things. Fertile soil doesn't just happen on its own. Farmers add nutrients, rotate crops and ensure that the land is constantly revitalised. In the best cases, these changes happen in parallel with changes in tastes and markets to everybody's benefit. So, for example, growing pulses such as lentils and beans helps enrich the earth on the farm – but, thanks to the growth of vegetarian and vegan cuisine and its provision of vital proteins and nutrients for those diets, pulses also have an elevated status in the modern market.

THE HARVEST: SUCCESS GROWN FROM
THE RIGHT ENVIRONMENT

A company's success, its moment to enjoy the yield, is the harvest. But just as a farmer knows the work is not done when the crops are harvested, neither is the work of a business leader complete when profits are up. In fact, the work has only just begun. The soil must be prepared for the next cycle, enriched with new ideas and tended to with diligence.

The most successful companies – those that continue to grow, year after year – are those whose leaders understand the importance of maintaining fertile soil. They invest in their culture, their people and their processes. They understand that success is not a one-time achievement but the result of constant cultivation.

Young entrepreneurs can help us build a better future

There is opportunity to be had in difficult times when the old ideas are malfunctioning and people are more open to change

A jobs drought, a new academic year in which university fees will be more expensive than ever before and the first year-on-year decrease in upper A-level grades in memory. On the face of it, the situation for school leavers in Britain today seems particularly grim.

But I'm an optimist – I wouldn't have started a company in a recession or had the conviction to keep it going in the early, scary days, if I wasn't. And because of that, I believe that what seems like a time of shrinking horizons and prospects for the young could also be one of opportunity. And that it should be.

When the system is stuttering and the comforts and options people recently took for granted suddenly feel endangered or outdated, caution and conservatism get the upper hand. Understandably but disastrously, firms and policies are often ruled by fear, while individuals can be less eager to give young blood a chance, being focused on preserving their own positions.

But times like this are about change, which is why they should also be about new opportunities. People are open to new ideas when the old ones are plainly malfunctioning. We're more likely than usual to question our bad habits and inherited assumptions when circumstances shake us out of our comfort zone. When the preordained social and educational destinies our young people anticipated are denied them, it should be an opportunity to remember what we too often forget: under-21s are not just prospective employees or students, they are entrepreneurs too. But booming business cultures in emerging economies seem to be much better at celebrating and encouraging youthful energy and innovation than the establishment.

It goes without saying that Sir Richard Branson, Steve Jobs, Bill Gates, Larry Page, Sergey Brin and Mark Zuckerberg are unique and prodigiously clever, but the shared virtue of their youth had plenty to do with their successes too. Not long out of their teens, but before they're fully entangled in the obligations of adulthood, people challenge convention and raise questions about the received wisdom of the world. Without a vested interest in maintaining the status quo or anything to lose, more interested in finding their own way than being ruled by others' expectations, young people are freer and better informed than anybody to think about building a better future.

One of the things that has most mattered to me in the years of my company AKQA, which I founded at 21, is nurturing the hungry, hopeful spirit we were created in. Of course, every motivational scheme, every brilliant new digital service that youth culture popularised, and every Virgin, Apple or Facebook also took investment, sacrifice and time. We know that funding can be hard to come by, and people are understandably anxious about taking on more debt to chase a dream, but in the digital world, more than ever before, you can start from a small base and low cost, and you can deliver a great idea.

If your work or ideas are good enough, you can quickly impress and connect to the right people via the digital channels, or you can put a great idea out there on a crowdfunding site such as Kickstarter and ask people to share your excitement to make it a reality. There's more scope than ever to see it as a means to a better end than a dead end, and use spare time to practically dedicate yourself to working out what you have that the world needs, and making it happen.

Today, as London 2012 amply demonstrated, we cherish and crave hope, excitement and people with the love and drive to realise their dreams. People who embody those virtues reconnect us with our own deepest feelings and desires.

One thing digital will never change is the fact that entrepreneurialism demands genuine enthusiasm, belief and a willingness to contribute. It's also about encouraging our communities to amplify strengths and have faith in their insights.

— This feature was originally published in The Guardian *in August 2012 —*

IT'S
EASIER
DONE
~~THAN~~
~~SAID.~~

The best
work is
created in
a state of
complete
devotion.

Good work carves a crevice in your synapses.

IF WE STOP BEING BETTER, WE STOP BEING GOOD.

A SETBACK COULD CONTAIN THE SEEDS OF SUCCESS

AS OUR GREATEST TRIUMPHS CAN RISE FROM OUR MOST HUMBLING DEFEATS

Why exchange good For new ?

WE HAVE NEVER STOPPED BEING

BEING

STUDENTS

We want people
nodding along   f
not nodding off f

f

f

f

f

The most powerful
force in the universe
isn't technology,
or imagination.

It's love.

2

When Creativity Meets Technology

Artists have always needed tools.
In the era of intelligent machines, the
real trick is to keep hold of the human

Has AI lost the plot? Or is it just waiting for the right story?

ARTIFICIAL INTELLIGENCE, AUTHENTIC CHARACTER: FROM SIRI TO C-3PO, I, ROBOT AND YOU

Character is plot, and plot is character. That truth goes back to Aristotle and still holds in any worthwhile tutorial for writing a story.

The theory goes that if your characters don't have compelling desires, and those aims aren't complicated by crisis and adversity, your stories will fail to captivate an audience.

As tech behemoths and babies battle it out to win the supreme share of an AI future, it's an insight we should keep in mind.

Though they have names, today's AIs are presented less as characters and more as abstract oracles. Despite our awareness of AI's nonhuman nature, we cannot resist anthropomorphising them, as evidenced by children befriending Alexa and adults selecting Siri's voice based on a penchant for algorithmic authority. This doesn't mean we should tolerate a future in which bots reply with errors or spectacular meltdowns (forgive the AIs, for they know not what they do). Nor does it mean we have to pretend a piece of tech is a person.

Instead, if we accept artificial intelligence (AI) is what it says – a fiction, a programmed performance of 'intelligence' – it follows that there's only one way to escape the 'uncanny valley' altogether: with character.

When it comes to the interplay between personality and AI, we are dealing with a creature, not a bug. Or, as poet Samuel Taylor Coleridge observed two centuries ago, fables demand a "human interest" that lets us willingly suspend disbelief and immerse ourselves in the tale – surrender to the story.

As glitches are fixed, the AI playing field will shift towards valuing personality over eradicating it. We've already had 'virtual assistants' and 'intelligent agents'. The inevitable next step would be the introduction of a versatile 'partner AI' that, much like a capable private secretary or concierge, can adeptly handle intricate tasks and anticipate individual needs and unique preferences: less a neutral backstage facilitator, more a continual presence in your life's next chapter.

We don't mistake the iconic AIs of the movies for people, but we know they have personalities, and we have our favourites just the same.

Feeling stuck and hopeless? Look to curious, compassionate and spiritual Samantha from 'Her'. Want a good angel on your shoulder, so you don't do something silly? Summon C-3PO. Need a bit more devil? Say hello to HAL. When your diary demands heroism, but you don't feel up to it, turn to J.A.R.V.I.S. for courage and calm.

Perhaps cinema's most beloved is Teddy from the film *A.I. Artificial Intelligence*. Embodying a deep sense of devotion, Teddy is warm, and wise. His motivations arise from his coding as a sidekick and protector, but he will grouch if you call him a 'toy'.

In a complex world that often feels chaotic and uncertain, Teddy's nurturing spirit makes him the ultimate mentor and guide: the best of what it means to be human, even if he isn't one.

— First published in March 2023 —

Art without artists

Why AI can't paint the full picture

LOST IN TRANSLATION — CAN ART AND ALGORITHMS CONVERSE?

When artists and technologists debate the relationship between AI and art, one of the biggest issues is that they are often trying to have a conversation in two different languages. The artist invokes concepts like 'imagination', 'authenticity', 'soul' or 'the human condition'; the scientifically minded critic counters that these are at best vague terms and at worst delusions that ignore what neuroscience and biology teach us about the human mind. Even 'consciousness' is the subject of centuries of scientific and philosophical dispute.

But science also tells us that humans are mammals and that our brains are not cold, calculating machines but organs powered by the blood in our veins and the air that we breathe, making choices powered by love and fear, hunger and desire. As such, the notion that we can mechanically dismantle and digitally recreate the workings of the human artist is just another fairy story.

THE RATIONAL ILLUSION: WHY HUMANS ARE NOT MACHINES

The argument that we are 'rational' creatures suggests that our thought processes should be easily replicable by technological means. But 'rationality' is a term derived from accountancy and mathematical logic, and a word that in the 20th century supplanted the older and more nuanced concept of 'reason'. 'Rationality' was a useful story about ourselves that took hold for good reasons – scarred by the delusions and destructive ideologies that powered two unimaginably damaging world wars, politicians saw technocracy as a measured, balanced way to ensure such horrors didn't happen again. Similarly, as business schools and economic theory blossomed after World War II, the notion that humans act in 'rational self-interest' became a way to assert the superiority of consumer choice over top-down totalitarian rule.

At the same time as economists publicly expounded the fable of rational self-interest, the smartest businesses and leaders demonstrated an ongoing respect for the importance of the irrational. Why else would a nephew of Sigmund Freud, enlisted by the US government, be credited with changing citizens' minds about entry into the first World War before going on to invent the discipline of public relations? Why else would the psychometric tests used to profile applicants for important executive roles have their origins in Carl Jung's ideas about psychological archetypes?

Humans aren't rational – certainly not all the time – and that's surely why art exists at all. Many anthropologists propose that art developed from ritual and that it emerged from the emotional experiences of individuals and small communities, from love and loss, triumph and tragedy, joy and uncertainty. That it's a way for us to give shape to experiences which are ineffable and irrational.

CODE WITHOUT SOUL: THE VOID OF 'CREATIVITY' LACKING LIVED EXPERIENCE

By contrast, artificial intelligence (AI), however sophisticated, lacks this inner world and the urge to express it. Its creations are born not of lived experiences but of web scraping, algorithms and logic. This might be analogous to the way human-made artworks come from particular personal and historical contexts, but it's not the same thing. Of course, AI can 'do' technical brilliance and aesthetic precision, but its output cannot stem from the motivation behind human art, which is to give shape to thoughts and feelings that can't be rendered simply as data or information.

THE SERENDIPITY OF CREATIVITY: HOW ART BEGINS WHERE SYSTEMS FAIL

You can't legislate for irrationality and serendipity – for those unexpected turns, mistakes and leaps of intuition that defy logic and predictability and flourish beyond the boundaries of reason. An AI can knock up a piece of visual art, or even a novel, in the blink of an eye. But it's striking how often you hear a painter or a writer talk about a famous work that sat gathering dust for years before – informed by a chance encounter, reawakened memory, or change of mood – they returned to it armed with a new connection or perspective that enabled them to make it work. It's also striking how often, in today's streamer-led cultural landscape, people use 'content' in a pejorative way, to characterise art that feels like it may as well have been made by AI – generic and predictable writing, film audio or visual art that seems to exist for no great intent or impetus beyond filling a slot in an upload schedule.

AI, for all its 'god-like' power, operates within the confines of its programming, unable to truly replicate the spontaneity and creative risk-taking that give rise to innovation. What it produces may simulate unpredictability, but it remains tethered to predetermined systems and frameworks. Human artists create with purpose, even when that purpose is not clear to themselves. (Again, how often do you hear a poet or novelist say they don't know what they think until they begin writing, revising or starting sentences whose endings mysteriously materialise?) AI lacks any equivalent intention. It does not 'mean' anything by what it generates, for it exists without the ability to feel. Yes, it can tell a story, according to the rules of Hollywood beat sheets or Aristotelian poetics. But it cannot imbue its creations with narrative resonance.

FROM ATELIER TO AI — A NEW RENAISSANCE FOR COLLABORATIVE CREATION?

Great Renaissance artists like Rembrandt and Rubens had scores of assistants and pupils trained to emulate their personal styles. Many of the best-known conceptual artists of our age also have teams who work to realise their works, just as novelists are increasingly employing AI to help them realise stories and styles that speak to our cultural moment. Perhaps this is the best way to understand AI, with its dependence on preordained parameters and definitions of what art is and its potential contribution to creative work.

REDEFINING ART IN THE AGE OF DIGITAL PRODUCTION

It goes without saying that AI has massive power and potential as a tool, a collaborator that amplifies human creativity rather than replaces it. If human artists can treat it as an ally rather than a threat to their vocation, it can help them do what groundbreaking art always does: renew our wonder at the world, reset our assumptions about creativity and compel us to redefine what we mean by 'art' in the first place.

Britain's creative industries are essential to the economy, but imagination must shape all our businesses

Let's start with the good news. The UK economy is set to grow by six per cent in 2022. Admittedly, this forecast, set by the Office for Budget Responsibility, was before we knew about the COVID-19 Omicron variant. But we must remain optimistic that the economy can continue to bounce back from the shockwave of the virus. When we think about the fuel that will power our economic growth, our creative flair will be absolutely crucial.

The UK's creative industries are one of the country's great strengths. According to figures, the cultural and creative industries contributed £115 billion to the economy in 2019, corresponding to six per cent of GDP. They account for almost 12 per cent of the UK's international exports. British brands such as James Bond, Harry Potter, Kingsman and, of course, Peppa Pig, have a global following. Creative fields such as film, TV, books, music and fashion give the UK global reach.

Creativity is the act of turning imagination into reality, delivery and action. But we must not delegate creativity solely to those sectors. The value of creativity to the UK economy, for people in all businesses and industries, is immeasurable. The degree of creativity in different businesses, however, is extremely variable. Although some organisations embrace the power of creativity, other more traditional organisations suppress the imagination of employees.

There are different ways that businesses quash and stifle creativity. From micromanaging to budgeting time and resources, how a company manages its employees defines the level of creativity in a business.

A company may play it safe, rejecting ideas as they break or stretch the traditional way the business has operated. One example is the virtue-signalling, sententious worthiness that's seemingly the parlance of so much of today's banal advertising work. This homogeneity litters the landscape with easily forgotten communication clichés that blend into one another.

It is incumbent on CEOs to encourage creative behaviours in employees. They must break with traditional thinking patterns to have fresh ideas.

It is also essential to create new and unexpected connections. Some of the best perspectives and ideas occur almost by chance and could be sparked by talking to someone with a different mindset because of their life experience, age or cultural background or by applying the creativity from one industry to another. Powered by renewable energy, Tesla is consistently one of the highest-selling automotive brands, and its success is fuelled by innovation capital that's transformational and inspiring. The extraordinary number of new ideas in each Tesla vehicle, such as autopilot and the 'sentry mode' surveillance system, make it easy to see why. People may feel comfortable with the familiar, but they are aroused by the new.

As we navigate our way out of the trials and tribulations of COVID-19, creativity will be an even more important attribute. The World Economic Forum has already recognised it as one of the top five skills for the future. The pandemic has accelerated the prevalence of technology in the workplace. AI and robotics will further disrupt the world of work. Several surveys show that more than half the job descriptions we'll be using in 2030 have yet to be defined. The march of technology will not diminish the importance of creativity but enhance it.

Creativity is an essential part of our economic and technological future. It's easy to speak about creativity, but businesses all too often hinder and hamper it by playing it safe. Both businesses, large and small, in all areas of the economy, must encourage their employees to reject traditional thinking, make new connections and gain new perspectives. If we allow it to flourish throughout the economy, creativity will certainly be a catalyst for boundless innovation and reinvigoration.

— First published in City A.M. *on 21 December 2021 —*

Why resisting ease is the path to digital excellence

High achievement comes from persistence, not convenience, as exemplified in Ang Lee's use of 3D in *Life of Pi*

It takes little time for Ang Lee's *Life of Pi* to make you forget you're at the movies wearing 3D glasses. Instead, it convinces you that – for a second – you are in the presence of magic. In the opening moments of the film, a hummingbird appears to escape from behind the big screen and dart around the cinema. It's a glimpse of the wonders to come, but it's also a bold statement of intent from a brilliant director.

In the original novel, the narrator says Pi's story is so miraculous that hearing it turned him from an unbeliever to a believer. When he decided to adapt it for the screen, Lee evidently wanted to do something similar for his audience. To do justice to the transformative power of this wondrous tale, Lee had to find a way to make a boy talking to an animal on a raft floating on the open sea cinematically compelling. In settling on the right solution, Lee achieved a miracle of his own: he made people believe in 3D again. In his hands, 3D was not a gimmick demanded by marketing suits, but a conceptual cornerstone and technical foundation of the film. It's a lesson media professionals should take to heart.

The film's editor Tim Squyres had to imagine everything would come together in a compelling 3D experience: "Visual effects and 3D are really hard. Everything's much harder. 2D is a lot more forgiving – even just with simple blue screens … If there's something you have to paint out in 2D, it's nothing. In 3D, you have to have the whole space mapped and track it equally in both eyes, so it takes 20 times as long. Things that are relatively simple in 2D are a nightmare in 3D."

THE EASIEST ROUTE IS RARELY THE BEST ONE

In digital, we creators endure nightmares to ensure the audience experience is, for them, a dream. Perhaps in the pursuit of excellence, that's the way it will always be. Digital has made so many things that were once the domain of a few specialists accessible and achievable by many – creating exceptional work today demands great discipline. The easiest route is rarely the best one. Digital has amplified this tendency, but down the centuries, great engineers, artists and craftspeople have always known that nothing worthwhile comes easy.

Besides Lee, the directors doing most to set 3D free are two of the greatest auteurs of our age. Peter Jackson – who made the first ever motion picture to run at 48 frames a second in order to enhance realism and improve 3D – is refusing to compromise his vision to appease doubters who wanted to take the familiar route. Visionaries tend to take the long view.

Consider Alex Moulton, a great British engineer who died in December 2012 at the age of 92. Moulton's expertise could be traced back three generations, to the founding of his family's rubber business. But when that company was bought out in the late 1950s, Moulton founded his own firm, Moulton Developments Limited. There, he applied his deep knowledge of the material to help develop a new kind of suspension system that occupied less space yet enabled a smooth ride on small wheels and made the Mini a roadworthy reality.

A couple of years later, Moulton developed his unrivalled insight into suspension, tyre pressure and rubber to help invent another form of transportation: the small-wheeled commuter bike, with a one-size-fits-all frame and a cushioning suspension system, hailed in its day as the biggest leap in bicycles since the penny-farthing. His friend and champion James Dyson said after his death that Moulton's life showed how huge a culture influence you could have by relentlessly refining a very specific skill. "He stuck to two very finite fields – suspension and bicycles – in which he became the world's expert. There's an important lesson for us in that; sticking to one thing leads to a place nobody else can get to."

Today, the world's most acclaimed restaurant is Copenhagen's Noma. But for years after it opened in 2004, head chef René Redzepi lived on next to nothing to make his dream restaurant stay afloat. Even now, he still sees excellence and suffering as interconnected: "The restaurant industry is brutal: you work your arse off; you worry about bookings and gross profit and larder management.

So waking up after way too little sleep and going out into the countryside and eating these wild herbs and experiencing these subtle, brittle flavours, forces you to engage with the world around you as a cook."

The challenge for the rest of us is to do something similar: resist ease to create excellence. The sleepless nights are all worth it when the end result emerges and you succeed in pushing things forward. Athletes often talk about their most ecstatic moments being when they're rewarded with a win after giving their all. In business, people don't tend to talk this way, but it's the same human energy and endeavour that's being applied, just on a different pitch.

There's a great interview with Francis Ford Coppola talking about *Apocalypse Now* in 1979, when it was still seen as the biggest turkey ever. The interviewer asks him whether he panicked about spending so much on his dream project. Coppola says no. Money was something he could get back later as a director-for-hire, but a movie was something he'd only have one shot at doing as well as possible. As such, it wasn't a sin to risk and invest everything in a film he believed in – instead, it would have been a sin not to: "I believe that film-making… is a game you should play with all your cards, and all your dice, and whatever else you've got. So, each time I make a movie, I give it everything I have. I think everyone should, and I think everyone should do everything they do that way."

— First published in The Guardian *in February 2013 —*

Changing the rules of the game

Now bigger in size than Hollywood and with the potential to become an even greater storytelling medium, the video game industry could end up as the ultimate marketing platform

In an otherwise unremarkable day in early March, something truly extraordinary happened. Having sold more than 25 million copies of its blockbuster title *Halo 3*, the game creator Bungie announced that at precisely 6:36 p.m., in a three-minute-and-19-second online game, four players (separated by physical distance but not by purpose) participated in *Halo 3*'s one-billionth match. If every multiplayer game of *Halo 3* lasted only around three minutes – mirroring this one – the total duration of all gameplay would be more than 63 centuries, 630 decades or 6,300 years. By anyone's reasoning, that's a lot of time.

If ever an illustration were needed to articulate that – like books, film or television before them – video games are the new medium of our age and an awesome, still-burgeoning phenomenon of our culture, this was it. Video games are even being taken seriously in some surprisingly noncommercial quarters: university sociology and anthropology departments are offering courses on the significance of electronic games in society, and the web is rife with references to doctoral dissertations written about gaming and its influence on culture.

What makes video games so remarkable is how they combine the audiovisual capabilities of film, human insights from great literature, unlimited creative possibilities of animation and an interactivity utterly unique to the genre.

Given the craftsmanship that goes into today's best titles and the interactive storytelling and atmospheric immersion they enable, video games are arguably a new art form.

As Henry Jenkins of MIT argues, video games can "generate aesthetically and socially meaningful experiences which communicate complex ideas in a rich way", as well as offering a path beyond the static narrative which even the greatest of writers have at times found confining.

Take the astonishing perspective Jenkins offers regarding the epic book *War and Peace*: "Could a game be as good a work as *War and Peace*?" he asks. "It might be a better work…video games are going to do what literature has long wanted to do…we are certainly still in that trajectory."

An emerging generation of game designers and publishers is convinced that video games are the ultimate storytelling medium. They are also big business. In terms of size, the video game industry is now mightier than Hollywood. Game developers measure success not only by the volume they sell or the income generated but also by the total duration of gameplay offered by their stable, which varies from a few minutes to several hours. And because brands – most of the great ones, anyway – are about stories and emotional involvement, video games may also evolve to become the ultimate marketing platform.

There is always fear and loathing of any new medium. There was even a time when reading novels or going to the cinema were regarded as frivolous wastes of time. That's also possibly the mainstream view of videogaming today.

Mass consumer acceptance, combined with a huge diversity of titles, however, signals that we are already entering a new 'age of play', and given that play is the fountain of creativity, then video games surely represent a new addition to the media landscape and a heavenly match for brands.

Many respected schools teach game design from an artistic, multidisciplinary perspective and a new generation born with sophisticated games as an intrinsic, natural and accepted part of their culture doesn't take issue with the idea of a game being a form of creative expression.

Let's also enlist John C. Beck and Mitchell Wade and their book *Got Game*: "Anyone who actually looks at the games selling and being played knows that the typical video game is not the blood-splattering, media-grabbing, parent-stressing cartoon that makes the nightly news on a slow or tragic day. Instead, it's a massive problem-solving exercise wrapped in the veneer of an exotic adventure. Or it's the detailed simulation of an entire civilisation, or a pivotal battle that affected the course of world history. Or it's a serious opportunity to try coaching a sports team or setting military strategy. In short…games…lead the brain to new combinations of cognitive tasks and demand new levels of processing power."

Indeed, by occupying our minds so robustly, video games can not only be good for us, they can really make us feel things, enrapture us and help us conjure that wonderful psychological state known as 'flow'. The operative concept here is *compelling*, and the fact that video games are so compelling is why, despite being in many ways still a relatively nascent medium, perhaps somewhere about where film and music were 40 or 50 years ago, they are already a huge space for advertising.

In-game advertising spend was up 40 per cent in 2008 while conventional media spend was going sideways. Marshall McLuhan noted that "the medium is the message" and what better way to show that the new administration is in touch with technology, trends and the people than by Barack Obama's team placing media spend ads into games (including *Burnout Paradise* and *Madden NFL 09*) in 10 'battleground states' just weeks before election day?

For the moment, in-game advertising works a lot like product placement spots in films and sits at a similar level of sophistication. The cardinal rule of video game marketing today is that brand messages should not interfere with your fun. This is why ads on hoardings in football games or on billboards and the sides of taxi cabs in hits such as *Grand Theft Auto* are credible: they give the player the chance to explore and bump into the brand, and because we are surrounded by logos and straplines in everyday life, they enhance the realism of the game. Numerous surveys prove that gamers see it this way also and overwhelmingly enjoy brands' infiltration into the virtual world.

One reason marketers like in-game advertising is because it rewards those who don't get in the way of the game-playing. And in the on-demand reality of the world we live in, advertising that respects its audience is essentially the only form that really grabs anyone's attention. Ever-better graphics, sound and playability, meanwhile, will continually raise the bar for how smart an advertiser has to be to create an effective in-game commercial or branded experience; it's going to require more, not less, thinking as video games increasingly evolve into digital worlds that people inhabit for longer and longer.

What happens down the line, when consuming electronic stories has become second nature for the majority of the population, is not self-evident. Accordingly, to envision the future of video game advertising, you can't just extrapolate from how Omega or Sony Ericsson use the latest James Bond film to peddle expensive watches or mobile handsets. You have to close your eyes and try to imagine how a brand we don't know about yet, or a product or service we're not currently able to conceptualise, might promote itself using the evolving video game medium in a totally novel way.

Luckily, we haven't long to wait for some answers. Until now, gaming has been the domain of the manufacturers of the major consoles and the software developers who make them. But this paradigm is disintegrating as we speak.

Electronic distribution is shaking up the old retail markets, and indie programmers are already taking game development out of the hands of the long-dominant 'studio system' (which, like its Hollywood counterpart, traditionally favours shallow action titles). The depth and variety as well as the storytelling power and finer audience segmentation of available games will be enhanced by this trend.

Most disruptive of all, though, is the fact that, in the words of Rob Fahey at gamesindustry.biz: "Mobile devices have become powerful enough to rival handheld game consoles. Led by Apple, the rise of smartphone gaming looks set to be inexorable in 2009."

Social networking and gaming are also becoming intertwined. This will be followed by the progressively and insistently more complete intermingling of the virtual and the real, of the online and the offline, of our work and our play.

But the fact remains that as marketing clutter increases and media continues to fragment, advertising is running out of space in the most important medium of all: the human mind. We are learning more and more every week about the psychological and physiological impact of the media that inundates and stimulates us daily from dawn till well past dusk. On balance, the influence is positive as people are more empowered with access to knowledge and information. More intriguing, though, is the mounting evidence that neuroplasticity – the capacity of neural pathways to readjust once formed – is greater than formerly thought and that human beings are able to continually optimise our brains throughout our lives. What this means is that some video games will have, or may already have, the power to make us better people.

So how are all these forces, from social networking to science, relevant to marketing through video games? Well, as has always been true, the brands that get the most will be the ones that give the most: those that make us laugh, feel better about ourselves, that genuinely inspire us and make our lives better as individuals and as groups. In the case of video games, the winning brands will be those that harness the full potential of the medium – graphical, neurological or cultural – to deliver something truly fantastic to a waiting world that doesn't know it's waiting.

Among other emergent trends, there will be more instances of what the Oxford professor Douglas Holt describes as authentic cultural branding, where brands earn their keep by playing an active and helpful role in a global, national or subculture. In Holt's model, "As cultural activists, managers treat their brands as a medium – no different than a novel or a film – to deliver provocative creative materials that respond to society's new cultural needs." So imagine, if you will, Tolstoy (or at least Stephen King) being the author of a brand and using the interactive medium of a video game as their chosen mode of expression. The effect will be more profound than today's in-game billboards – you can bet on that – and the marketing results will make banner ads seem as old school as the early arcade game *Pong*. From the perspective of the player, creator and brand, that makes everyone a winner.

— First published in Campaign *magazine in May 2009 —*

AI, cinema
and creativity

The human imperfection that machines can't mimic

Remember 2022, when ordinary people first got their hands on polished, powerful tools for AI-generated graphics and words, like Midjourney in July, and ChatGPT in November? Over the following year, opinion on the technology seemed to divide into two camps: those who thought the technology would end life as we know it on the one hand, and those who thought it was here to save us on the other. In that time, we all also read hundreds of newspaper columns by creative types about how AI and algorithms would never replace human imagination, which ironically tended to follow such a predictable pattern that they could have been written by AI.

Maybe they'll make a movie about it one day.

BUREAUCRACY VS CREATIVITY: AI'S DOUBLE-EDGED SWORD

Today, the popular discourse around the role of AI in modern life seems to have settled into a less dramatic groove. We've adapted to the fact that, in some areas, it's a fact of life. In finance, education, medicine – anywhere you have to process thousands of sets of data or filter through vast numbers of applicants to meet specific numbers – it's already part of the furniture. In such cases, AI is basically doing 'bureaucracy'.

This shouldn't necessarily be a bad thing. After all, 'bureaucracy' is a word which, properly used, means the standardisation of routine tasks in the name of efficiency. In the pejorative way we use it in everyday life, it means an organisation caught up in system over mission or a job so mindless and repetitive that it makes you feel like a machine.

But one industry where fears and fierce protests about AI still rage is the world of film and TV. And for good reason: for business, every crisis is an opportunity, and while the five-month Hollywood writers strike of 2023 eventually saw human talent win better terms, it also meant that the industry accelerated its efforts to incorporate AI into its processes.

In pre- and post-production, in the generation of translations and captions, AI saves time and money and has already supplanted roles that humans used to do. Studios are using AI to process scripts or to run the numbers on the likely box-office impact of casting this or that star. But these were always numerical decisions because show business is a business. Film funding has always been conditional on getting the right talent; on reshooting endings that don't meet with approval at test screenings; and on rewrites that cater to the average crowd over the original, individual creative impulse.

CAN DATA MAKE A BLOCKBUSTER?

When it comes to the alchemy of creating great, resonant movies and television, however, AI can't do it all and won't be able to any time soon. This is not because of some vague superstition about the sanctity of human creativity. This is because making film and TV is expensive, and those putting up the funds have always, naturally, sought to get any solid data they can about the likelihood of a project ending up a success. But the mysterious business of making a hit or a classic has never been reducible to past performance, statistical probabilities or future projections – hence the surprise hit or the epic flop. In the famous words of the screenwriter William Goldman's book *Adventures in the Screen Trade*, "Nobody knows anything… Not one person in the entire motion picture field knows for a certainty what's going to work. Every time out it's a guess and, if you're lucky, an educated one."

The most seasoned studio executives – armed with decades of experience, market research and gut instinct – regularly bet millions on films that fail. Meanwhile, projects rejected by every major studio sometimes become cultural phenomena. This isn't just cinema's problem. It's the fundamental paradox at the heart of all creative enterprises. Marketing departments spend fortunes trying to predict consumer behaviour. Entrepreneurs and investment groups develop detailed business plans. Creative directors make intuitive judgement calls founded on decades of experience. Yet the relationship between input and outcome remains stubbornly unpredictable. Even with data, experience and expertise, the creative process is inherently uncertain.

It requires a kind of humility in leadership – a recognition that being risk-averse, formulaic and predictable isn't going to cut through. It also necessitates an embracing of uncertainty. Remaining open to experimentation often proves more valuable than clinging to the illusion of control.

Today, streaming is so entrenched in our lifestyles that we forget how snooty the movie and TV establishment was about it until only a decade ago. The single most important production in changing perceptions of streaming drama was *House of Cards*. Through the series, Netflix made its reputation as a producer of original prestige drama. The official line the company promoted after its success was that they were a new kind of digital age studio, and the series was a new kind of digital age hit: not a serendipitous or lucky beneficiary of the stars aligning, but rather a carefully calculated success, driven by subscriber data. Their sophisticated algorithms, so the story went, identified the exact formula for a show that audiences couldn't resist: compelling political drama; a starry, cinema–grade cast; and oversight by director–producer David Fincher: voilà, a smash hit was born. For a moment, it seemed like Netflix had cracked the code.

THE MYTH OF THE ALGORITHMIC HIT

This story did a great job of promoting Netflix as a new kind of content platform, but it ignored some inconvenient details. *House of Cards* was an adaptation of an old BBC series, an already acclaimed story originally written by a political aide and then adapted for the Netflix version by a writer who also had direct, human experience of the inner workings of political campaigning. It wasn't developed in a petri dish but at a production company. Netflix, aware of the value an intelligent drama would have to their image, outbid established networks to secure rights to the show. Their most crucial calculation was understanding how opinion and expert approval would elevate the second-tier reputation that streaming had. Gushing critical approval and breakthrough success at awards ceremonies like the Emmys proved them right.

It was a compelling story told on the back of a compelling story. But it was barely less fictional. After all, if data alone can produce TV gold, why doesn't Netflix have every widely celebrated smash hit series right now? If the narrative about *House of Cards* had been entirely true, Netflix would be an unstoppable factory of success, churning out hit after hit. But reality tells a different tale. Netflix's track record is far from flawless. For every *Stranger Things*, there are countless forgettable series and cancelled seasons. On paper and by the numbers, something like the 2024 Netflix series *3 Body Problem* looked bulletproof: based on a bestselling novel in the world's second most populous country, a novel which, when translated, became the winner of the USA's most prestigious sci-fi award, then adapted for screen by the duo behind the success of *Game of Thrones*. It had all the odds in its favour. Yet it doesn't seem to have clicked with the times or the global audience. So why can't data-driven insights guarantee consistent success in entertainment?

WHEN MACHINES MIMIC ART

Data may give you insights into what people like, but it can't manufacture the magic of storytelling. Creativity doesn't fit neatly into an algorithm. You can't legislate for success in entertainment. *House of Cards'* success came from its powerful performances, sharp writing and narrative that tapped into the cultural zeitgeist.

But you can't build the next hot hit by simply processing and profiling what worked before. Data can point to past successes, but it struggles to predict what will resonate in the future. Audiences evolve, and tastes shift, often unpredictably. What data can't grasp is the element of surprise. The truth is that the best and most compelling shows are often the ones that offer something unexpected.

Netflix likely didn't anticipate *Stranger Things* becoming the cultural phenomenon it did. The nostalgic, 80s-inspired sci-fi horror series was a risky bet, with relatively unknown child actors and in a genre hitherto seen as niche rather than part of the TV mainstream. Yet it became one of Netflix's biggest hits. Why? Because it offered something fresh, something data couldn't have predicted.

Adolescence, a more recent Netflix headline-maker, was another offering that triumphed despite data, not because of it. Rather than doing the bidding of algorithms or being pitched at entire advertiser-friendly audience demographics, the 2025 limited series connected because of its grounding in real lives. The heartbreaking true stories of real families were woven into its narrative of a murdered teenager. The creators' decision to capture each episode in a single take prioritised the ancient theatrical power of live performance over precisely programmed camera movements and expertly engineered plot twists. Thanks to those choices, the show broke UK streaming records and topped Netflix's Most Watched charts around the world.

Netflix is a pioneer. But today it is no longer the only player in the game. When *House of Cards* premiered, the streaming giant had little competition. Now, the landscape is far more crowded, with platforms such as Disney+, Apple TV+, Amazon Prime and HBO Max vying for audience attention. This increased competition means even well-crafted, data-backed shows can get lost in the noise.

One very real risk of making efficiencies with AI is that you end up with more content that is easier to make, leading to a deluge of overfamiliar shows that make everything seem like interchangeable (if expensive) slush, rather than standout must-sees. This is the paradox of data-driven creativity: it can help refine what works, but it can also lead to a lack of originality. The more content follows the same patterns, the less likely it is to stand out. Timing, luck and cultural context are as important as technical quality or the CVs of your team. A show that might have been a hit five years ago could easily be overlooked today.

David Fincher, one of the crucial architects of *House of Cards* and its elevation of the status of streaming TV, said of the type of still and moving images generated by generative AI software such as Midjourney and DALL-E that "it always looks like sort of a low-rent version of [revered cinematographer] Roger Deakins." When people talk about these kinds of learning AIs as 'stealing', they miss the point and the nature of the technology; Fincher, who is renowned for his attention to detail, hits on the real issue. By spotting and duplicating patterns in commercial art styles, popular genres and sales successes, AI art and video tend to fall into their own predictable patterns of frame composition and visual grammar – the opposite of what defines the kind of art that breaks through, amazes us, shocks us. As a rule, AI moving pictures look less like the future of film and more like a very slick new standard of clip art. The things brands and artists alike crave – a unique visual signature; an instantly identifiable identity – are what it is least equipped to output.

You can see this if you compare, say, the slew of short AI films made over the past year or two to *Sunspring*, an experimental 2016 project inspired by the victory of DeepMind's AI over the world's best player of the Chinese strategy game Go. *Sunspring* is a live-action, low-budget sci-fi film which uses a script generated entirely by a learning AI that had been fed hundreds of classic sci-fi scripts. The script it delivered was basically gibberish – barely a line in the film makes any referential sense – but the tension and atmosphere and the conviction with which it's performed and shot, give the whole thing a compelling aura and mystique. Despite the big-budget ad-campaign sheen of more recent productions, *Sunspring* has something that the slick, polished and coherent all-AI movies of today don't. It's strange. It's otherworldly. It's uncanny. But not in the bad, 'uncanny valley' sense that all-digital attempts to approximate reality often are; it's uncanny – a little spooky, a lot odd, a tad discombobulating – because of the earnestness and commitment with which its human actors perform the compelling, yet nonsensical, AI-made script.

Watching *Sunspring* today, then, is a reminder both of how far AI for filmmaking has come and of what we risk losing if we conflate technical competence and surface finesse with creativity itself. Many 'creatives' working in fields like commercial illustration and copywriting have valid fears about AI taking their jobs – but rather than prove that AI is truly artistic, this fact is really a reminder of how much 'creative' work isn't actually very creative.

I put 'creative' in quotation marks because in industries such as media and marketing, 'creative' is simply a description of a job role or a piece of work, not a judgement on the artistry of that work. Similarly, we use 'art-working' not as a description of somebody necessarily working on art, but someone technically fine-tuning a design which might have zero art to it, such as a voucher or a banner ad. There are clear rules to such designs, just as there is a standard language and idiom for copywriting and 'churnalism' and a standard artistic grammar for commercial imagery such as book covers or film posters.

The tendency to more of the same doesn't stop there. Often, the client doesn't want originality – they want what you did for the other company. Frequently, an agency itself doesn't pitch creativity – they pitch 'existing thing X combined with existing thing Y'. What we pass off as 'creative', in other words, is often no more artistic than a prompt for a text, movie or image bot. The more predictable our so-called creativity, the easier it is for machines to learn its rules and replace us. These once-human roles will be increasingly displaced by cheaper and quicker AI solutions, just as translators have already seen their work endangered, and scribes were surely panicked by Gutenberg's invention of a printing press for movable type almost 800 years ago.

If we're going to defend and nurture human creativity in the face of such developments, our energies are best expended not on doomed attempts to outlaw new technology but on remembering and reinforcing what creativity is. Until this point we've been talking about film – 'moving pictures', and that itself is a reminder that the medium of the movie might not have come into existence had creative minds not applied their ingenuity to the tools of still photography to create the illusion of motion (the first ever film, shot in the UK, moved at a mere seven frames per second). But let's for a moment consider still photography itself.

The invention of the camera in 1839 sparked fear among the painters of the time, who worried that their craft might become obsolete. Yet rather than replacing painting, the camera became another tool for artistic expression, not only coexisting with traditional art forms but also inspiring them. To give just one example, the Impressionist movement led by Monet in the 1880s was, in many ways, a response to the advent of photography. Artists no longer felt the need to replicate reality with precision – because the camera could do that. Instead, they explored light, emotion and abstraction, giving rise to a whole new way of seeing the world. Later, Picasso and his cubist peers would do something similar by painting portraits in which multiple viewpoints were combined in one image.

These examples express an age-old truth about humans: we have an extraordinary capacity to adapt, innovate and take massive leaps forward when faced with transformative technology.

Do I believe AI is an amazing tool, capable of replicating and even enhancing existing styles? Absolutely. But do I believe AI can make intuitive, groundbreaking leaps to create entirely new movements or styles that redefine creativity? No, not yet. Achieving that kind of innovation is undoubtedly an aspiration of those currently working on artificial general intelligence but for the moment, it remains only an aspiration.

CONTENT OR CULTURE? THE RISK OF AI HOMOGENISATION AND WHY ART NEEDS THE UNEXPECTED

In a world where artificial intelligence (AI) is often hailed as the pinnacle of innovation, some claim it will eventually surpass humans in all domains, including creativity. However, the idea of a 'cultural algorithm' – a system capable of encapsulating and reproducing human creativity – fundamentally misconstrues the nature of creativity itself. Creativity is inherently rooted in lived experiences, emotions and cultural nuances that algorithms, no matter how advanced, struggle to replicate authentically.

Take, for example, music. AI can generate compositions in the style of Beethoven or modern pop hits by analysing patterns in existing works. However, it lacks the emotional intent that drives original creativity. Beethoven's compositions were shaped by his hearing loss, his philosophical reflections and his personal tragedies. (And, like all arts, by the evolution of musical technology and of performance spaces; the piano and the concert hall were both developments that informed Beethoven, Mozart and what we now call 'The Classical period'.) AI may mimic these styles but cannot embody the profound human experiences that inspire them.

Similarly, in visual arts, AI tools can generate pieces reminiscent of famous painters, but they cannot create new artistic movements or challenge societal norms the way movements like Surrealism or Dadaism did. One of the current buzzwords in cutting-edge, processor-intensive video game graphics is 'ray-tracing' – the accurate simulation of the way light sources interact with three-dimensional space. It was invented by the great German painter Albrecht Dürer, over 500 years ago, with pieces of string.

Furthermore, creativity thrives on cultural context and individuality. A cultural algorithm, by definition, would homogenise output by relying on statistical generalities rather than individual, nuanced perspectives. Consider global cuisines: while AI might synthesise recipes by blending data from thousands of cultures, it cannot replicate the stories, rituals and memories that make food a cultural cornerstone and a springboard for memory. At best, AI creates variations on established themes, but it cannot introduce new paradigms that resonate on a deeply human level.

We are at a pivotal moment in the evolution of technology, where the promises of AI are immense, but its limits are also great. The hype around AI often neglects the fact that creativity is deeply tied to the human condition – our emotions, our struggles and our immense cultural diversity.

Creativity is a uniquely human response to the unpredictable. It comes from our ability to interpret the world through the lens of our experiences, challenges and emotions. AI can mimic, but we have seen no clear proof that it can originate. There's a risk that over-reliance on algorithms could lead to cultural stagnation, where the richness of human creativity is overshadowed by the uniformity of machine-generated outputs, and the ease of using digital presets, grids and bots makes it too easy to stay on the established path rather than go off the beaten track.

The good news about this, though, is that the more competent and quick AI becomes at replicating existing art, writing, music or photography and the more 'content' we output in standard formats, the greater our response to art that goes beyond competence and slickness. Art that speaks to us in the way art has since the first cave paintings: art that shakes us, moves us; art that reconnects us with the wonder and the mystery of human life. That's why we don't have to seek out starving artists to find what creativity should look like. We can simply go to the multiplex and savour the work of the pre-eminent visionary working in popular film-making today.

IMPROVISATION AND INTUITION – VILLENEUVE'S MASTERSTROKE

If you had a few hundred million dollars in your pocket today and you wanted to create a new marquee science fiction franchise, you wouldn't go to an AI. You wouldn't even go to George Lucas or Steven Spielberg. Chances are, you'd call Denis Villeneuve, the French–Canadian director who, in just four projects, has established himself as the leading creator of sweeping sci-fi films that combine modern technology and epic scale with intimate human drama. His breathtaking vistas and moments of cinematic magic are never just about spectacle for its own sake but always tie in with the family stories and emotional connections at the core of his drama. Thanks to their themes and to his deep interest in every facet of the filmmaking process, these films and his interviews about them are also uniquely illuminating projects for understanding the limits of AI's capacity for creating great moving pictures.

Villeneuve's first sci-fi success was 2016's *Arrival*. Its plot focuses on experts' attempts to translate an alien language and reflects on humans' frailty, mortality and sense of time by having its heroine interact with a species whose written communication makes no distinction between past and future. The film is an adaptation of a cerebral short story by Ted Chiang – the computer science graduate turned sci-fi author who today is *The New Yorker* magazine's go-to guy for articles on AI and creativity and whom *Time* magazine put on its 2023 list of The 100 Most Influential People in AI. In adapting Chiang's story, screenwriter Eric Heisserer was particularly challenged by the task of turning its bookish moments of linguistic decoding into gripping cinematic scenes. He found the answers from other people. First, out to dinner with his wife one night, he started making circular shapes with his fingers to explain how he was stuck trying to visualise the alien language – and she told him he'd just unwittingly demonstrated the answer: to transpose those shapes drawn in the air with his fingers into the alien language for the film. Villeneuve brought them to inky, atmospheric life in the film's most beautiful sequences. Next, when Heisserer gestured wildly in a conversation with colleagues about the difficulty of making exciting scenes out of the work of translation, he was told: use that. Make your characters show their excitement and frustration in the way you just did.

For his next project, *Blade Runner 2049*, Villeneuve and a host of talents (including the real Roger Deakins) revisited a beloved classic. To solve its greatest storytelling problem, Villeneuve turned not to code but to the Philip K. Dick novel on which the original was based, itself a rumination on the relationship between humanity and artificial intelligence. And in the movie's most beautiful and climactic scene, he went not for some explosive intergalactic crescendo but for the timeless, ancient wonder of snowfall and its power to connect experience across time and space, evoking the conclusion of James Joyce's most celebrated short story, 'The Dead', written a hundred years earlier: "Snow falling on everything, the living and the dead."

At the time of writing, after two successful instalments already released to great critical and commercial success, Villeneuve is working on the third and last of his adaptations of Frank Herbert's *Dune* novels, books he worshipped as a teenager who wanted to make movies when he grew up. The first two films have been object lessons in Villeneuve's ability to fuse what he calls 'intimacy and scope', emotion and technology; in them, family connections and enormous technological conflicts alike have been realised with his trademark scale and ethereal beauty.

Though the project hadn't yet been announced and wasn't mentioned by name, Villeneuve was already working on *Dune* in the autumn of 2017, when he went to Google to talk to DeepMind's founder Sir Demis Hassabis, before an audience of AI experts, for the launch of *Blade Runner 2049*. The reason he still liked real sets in our CGI age, he explained to Hassabis, is that they free actors to devote all their imagination to the life of their characters, rather than having to imagine a world that will be comped in after lonely work in front of a green screen. The reason that's valuable, he says, is that many of the greatest cinematic moments – just like the one in the original *Blade Runner* when Rutger Hauer releases a dove – evolved from improvisation. Improvisation happens when the performer feels fully 'in' the character and the character's world, rather than having to imagine it. Villeneuve and his team always leave space for improvisation by 'strong' actors, he explained, and there's nothing better than a morning when a performer comes in and says they've come up with an idea they really want to try. They go off-script, off-grid, off-piste and in doing so find something more authentic than any preset could generate. He compared it to the way the best moments in the best documentaries are moments that could not have been anticipated but are captured by the camera: "life itself creates a strong cinematic moment."

SIMULATING WEAKNESS: HUMANITY'S SECRET INGREDIENT

During the exchange, AI pioneer Hassabis asked Villeneuve about the role of AI in film-making: its potential and its limitations. Villeneuve, who is famous for the unusual degree of interest and exchange he has with every technologist, technician and artisan on his shoots, had a compelling answer.

"The complexity of humanity, that struggle to get rid of the voices that are coming from the past," he said. "That, I think you can't recreate with an AI." The unique experiences that make us, the "gift" of our particular way of seeing the world passed down by our parents and their parents and generations before: how, he wondered, do we create that? It was a fascinating thought, and no amount of pattern recognition, number crunching and computing strength can step in and take over if Villeneuve is right. If what makes us unique is not some fuzzy and scientifically suspect idea of "imagination", "consciousness" or even "creativity", but rather what Villeneuve went on to call "our weaknesses" Simulating that? He wondered, turning to Hassabis and the expert audience. "That's your problem."

The more rules you follow,
the fewer risks you take.

Exploration doesn't
thrive in a cage.

To

begin

again

is

not

to

start

over.

But

to

return,

more

awake.

Ideas must stand on their own merits and speak for themselves without the need for explanation or justification.

BE SERIOUS ABOUT THE WORK YOU DO.

(BUT DON'T TAKE YOURSELF TOO SERIOUSLY)

Let the
glory days
of story begin.

Lead by example, create examples that lead.

hand.

a

gives

and

us

in

believes

someone

when

ladder

the

up

rung

a

get

only

We.

It's a marathon and a sprint.

3

Beyond Business

Work to live, don't live to work.
Accomplishments amount to nothing if
you don't care about the wider world

Words can be enchanting, but there's no substitute for truthful action

Many companies talk about making the world better. Patagonia provides a solution, instead of more pollution. The new documentary *Wild Life* by Academy Award-winning film-makers celebrated for recording soaring triumphs of the human spirit is the story of the people behind Patagonia – a company that set standards for sustainability and environmental consciousness long before the concepts became mainstream.

The environment is such a daunting and difficult subject, and the work of Patagonia is so significant that the script could be more intimidating than inspiring.

Here, after all, is an unparalleled business that prioritises ecological growth over corporate growth by making products with maximum longevity and minimal impact in an industry known for wasteful practices.

Here is a company whose first CEO, Kristine Tompkins, retired from Patagonia to tackle the dual challenges of climate change and species loss, overseeing the rewilding and protection of over 15 million acres of land and 30 million acres of marine wilderness.

In other words, in other hands, the film's narrative might have made you feel inadequate and tune out rather than spur you to get out, sow seeds and scrutinise your supply chain.

But rather than frame its achievements as morally superior or shame the rest of us, Patagonia has a way of making its work sound less like high science or a lofty crusade and more like common sense. The heroic pursuit of conservation and regeneration is considered a form of 'rent' with which it's only fair to compensate the natural world for a stay on Earth.

Although we can't all be Patagonia, we can learn from its way of looking at things, like a refusal to see 'business' and 'planet-friendly' concerns as opposing forces. Pioneers such as health-tech giant Philips already report an environmental profit and loss analysis of what their business owes to nature.

New European legislation requires tens of thousands of companies to post their climate and societal impact data from 2024 to increase transparency and help combat corporate greenwashing.

Not every company can be Patagonia. But every organisation can be more responsible. The DNA of entrepreneurialism often rejects conventional business binaries by finding a new and improved way. A shift in perspective can take us beyond current dogma and limited confines to create lasting change.

There's still a mountain to climb, but there are countless reasons to be hopeful as long as we keep moving. As Kristine Tompkins says, we can't wait for the perfect moment, reminding us that despair – just like 'business as usual' – won't get us anywhere.

— First published in April 2023 —

The Commonwealth: 75 years of reinvention

On the 75th anniversary of the Commonwealth, it is imperative that we reassess the true value of this organisation – an asset often underestimated and overlooked amidst the political turmoil of recent years.

Brexit debates repeatedly relegated the Commonwealth to a mere bargaining chip, with arguments oscillating between its potential as a European Union substitute and its dismissal as a colonial relic. At its emergence in 1949, while the superpowers were intent on framing the postwar world as a game of Risk, the Commonwealth was closer to Happy Families. Yet these narratives fail to grasp the economic, geopolitical and technological potential a modern Commonwealth truly represents. Amidst a backdrop of conflicting accounts, it's unsurprising that outdated myths obscure the clarity of today's reality.

The Commonwealth is a voluntary association of 56 independent countries and is home to 2.5 billion people – almost a third of the world's population. It spans the six regions of Africa, the Americas, Asia, the Caribbean, Europe and the Pacific. It represents a fifth of the world's land mass and a quarter of the UN's membership, and more than a third of the planet's waters are under the national jurisdictions of Commonwealth members.

A global network connecting many of the fastest-growing nations, the combined GDP of Commonwealth countries is estimated to reach $20 trillion by 2027. True value often resides in the future potential of an asset, and foremost among the Commonwealth's assets is its useful population. More than 60 per cent are aged 29 or under – a demographic dividend teeming with potential for driving innovation that's primed to help reshape society and the global economy.

With its mosaic of nationalities spanning continents and cultures, the Commonwealth holds a wealth of ingenuity and instils a priceless sense of belonging. Through the shared values of the Commonwealth – encompassing democracy, human rights, equality, freedom of speech, justice, sustainable development, cultural diversity and security – members not only fuel dynamic conversations but also facilitate unified solutions.

Practical collaboration among the Commonwealth's 'family of nations' has surged at a time when many question its relevance and perceive the institution as languishing. Governments have nurtured some of this cooperation, while grassroots people-to-people communities, civil society and professional bodies participate quietly and without fanfare, through relationships underpinned with an unparalleled depth of independent networks and connections.

Numerous initiatives – such as trade facilitation, disease elimination and work to tackle climate change – have flourished. Throughout history, there's been a fixation on the geographic lines that separate us. But today's most pressing issues demand a shift in perspective. When environmental ruin strikes, it doesn't discriminate based on the imaginary boundaries devised by humans – and neither should we.

History also underscores the importance of courage and vision in driving progress. The Commonwealth has incubated transformative action and collective empowerment, from independence movements to social justice champions. Similarly, the challenges ahead, ranging from automation to economic stagnation and the urgent need for clean energy, necessitate collective action and inspiration across borders to address common problems.

Ethical leadership, scientific pursuit, entrepreneurial spirit, unity in diversity and equitable growth: All these drive global prosperity. Achieving a prosperous future requires robust, cooperative and multilateral relationships. The reservoir of human capital, unifying strength and cohesive influence of the Commonwealth has the potential to emerge as catalysts for progress and new industries. Given the brutality, divisiveness and unrelenting negativity reported across the media today, it's easy to adopt a cynical outlook. In reality, the future is always better than the past, even though it may not feel like that in the present. Pessimism is a prison that perpetuates itself by paralysing our will to act.

In the global arena, few nations possess the UK's unique convening power – a testament to credibility, relationships, geography, culture and history. As we navigate the complexities of the 21st century, the UK's role as a connector will be indispensable in shaping a more prosperous world. Britain excels when demonstrating its commitment to advancing the greater good, motivated by a desire to contribute positively to worldwide well-being. By convening and facilitating constructive dialogue across the Commonwealth, Britain plays a crucial role in fostering collaboration that benefits not only itself but also the broader international community. We mustn't settle for pomp, circumstance and ceremony without practical action.

Unlike other global organisations, the Commonwealth is not merely about economic gain. Its bonds of camaraderie and solidarity transcend the confines of geography and politics. It is about tapping into the collective wisdom and spirit of enterprise that flow through the people of the Commonwealth and channel these energies towards opportunity.

Having made it this far, the Commonwealth still demonstrates resilience, possibility and adaptability. Its appeal to prospective members embodies aspiration. But it also stands at a crossroads, with the choice between stagnation and revitalisation. In 2049, it will be a century old. Like any organisation that endures, it must stay true to its values and be forward-looking. Above all, the Commonwealth must constantly reinvent itself by giving the younger generation greater responsibility and opportunity.

— Written to mark Commonwealth Day, March 2024 —

We can't order a Menu of Conversation

But they can deliver us from awkward silences

People have always worried that the art of conversation is dying. But the right recipe always brings it back to life. Like writing letters or remembering birthdays before Google Calendar alerts, conversation is one of those old-fashioned things we sometimes wish we still did but which technology seems to have rendered ancient history.

Before this moment of hotshots, hot takes and hot-tempered online debates, before people worried that smartphones had killed conversation, they blamed TV. Before that, radio. In 1920, *Vanity Fair* ran an article entitled 'The Lost Art of Conversation' about the shameful banality of the average verbal exchange. In 1899, a piece again called 'The Lost Art of Conversation' in *The Saturday Evening Post* complained that people had forgotten how to talk to one another because they were all reading books or newspapers and "degenerating into unsocial silence." And way back in 1580, philosopher and essayist Montaigne wrote 'On Conversation', arguing this most stimulating dimension of interaction was routinely undervalued in favour of grander forms of debate.

It's consoling to look back and see that people have been worrying about conversation for centuries. A reminder that it was never effortless or 'natural' and always took thought. Today, some of the most interesting critics of culture don't just worry about the art of talking to each other; they provide tools to help us do it better and engage as individuals with unique stories that expand horizons instead of just being labelled enemies or allies.

Theodore Zeldin, the Oxford scholar who turns 90 in August, spares us the anxiety and embarrassment of not knowing where to begin. Zeldin advocates for empathetic exchanges that go beyond a safe space for small talk or easy banter, giving us the means to transform, challenge assumptions and explore perspectives by fostering understanding and talking about the fundamental concerns of our lives.

Whether working with titans or the timid, Zeldin's 'Conversation Menus' – a series of questions formulated to evoke insightful dialogue – offer food for thought during each course. A taster of the starter might be: 'How have your priorities changed over the years?' or 'How have your background and experience limited or favoured you?'

After chewing over some seriously weighty topics during the mains, 'How have you made and lost friendships, and what other kinds of friends would you like?' or 'If you were writing a book about your life, what would the title be and why?', dessert concludes with palate-cleansing questions such as, 'What do you think about your spending habits, and what do you need that money can't buy?'

We can find Zeldin's 'Conversation Menus' online or rustle up our own recipes. Like sitting down to a good meal, proper conversation can feel like a luxury we don't have time for. But when you do, it nourishes the soul in ways snack-sized chitchat never will.

— First published in May 2023 —

'The Future is in your hands.'

So why do young people sometimes feel like it's slipping through their fingers?

Today, half the world's population is under 30. They should shape all our tomorrows. It is often said that 'youth is wasted on the young'. In a way, it's true. While Earth's finite resources are plundered for short-term political fixes and greater economic gains for a smaller number of beneficiaries, one of the most valuable renewables – our planet's young people and their commitment to change – is undoubtedly being undervalued and underused.

Fifty-two per cent of the world's population is under 30, but that ratio rarely seems reflected in society's policy-making and governance. Whether it's a lack of representation or barriers to participation, young people are acutely aware of obstacles to involvement. The policies being pursued frequently fail to adequately or urgently address issues of concern – like climate change, conflict, career opportunities and the cost of living.

On the one hand, young people are often portrayed as being politically disengaged or apathetic. On the other, when they do take action to address challenges they feel can't wait, they're accused of impulsively intruding.

Part of addressing that gap is ensuring that the young feel enfranchised and empowered to exercise their democratic rights. But even then, today's democracy doesn't always seem to be doing its best for tomorrow's global inhabitants. It's hard to feel like a grown-up with an influential voice in the world when economic rewards and realities like decent pensions, property ownership and accessible healthcare seem elusive. Perhaps the only certainty is inheriting the mistakes of previous generations.

From microplastics and ultra-processed foods and their adverse effects on mind and body to the fossil-fuelled profits and power networks we're weaning ourselves off too slowly, the next wave can feel disempowered from determining their own destiny.

In premodern societies, where customs and cultures evolved to ensure the survival of the village and its tribe, a productive relationship between generations could be the difference between life and death. One of the crucial roles performed by the stewards of the present was to distil their perspective into wisdom they could pass on to the custodians of the future. It wasn't about individual rivalries or the squabbles of the day but about conveying a sense of the eternal cycle of life and helping equip a community's descendants for the untravelled path ahead.

The experiences and resilient optimism of today's young people radiate a distinct energy. If we rebuff their idealism and dismiss their fresh perspectives, it's not just their future we'll be risking. It's everyone's.

— First published in June 2023 —

A forgotten formula for better living: The Third Place

Dreams make better days. Third spaces shape better societies. Way back in 1989, when work was a physical location to which you went in the morning and clocked off in the evening, the sociologist Roy Oldenburg popularised the concept of the 'third place'.

Oldenburg characterised home as 'first place' and work as the second. The elusive 'third place' was his description of another kind of space where, liberated from the bonds and duties of your job and family life, you entered a neutral zone beyond everyday rules, roles and responsibilities – one where social status, earning power and privilege were left behind, and everybody entered on an equal footing.

Oldenburg argued that these convivial, conversational spaces were vital to the community, civic life and democracy itself. So perhaps it's no surprise that they look increasingly like endangered habitats in our polarised and unequal age. Pubs, cafés, places of worship, libraries, museums, galleries and parks: some of these locations have lost significance because of changes in the culture. Others have fallen victim to economic pressures.

Finding somewhere to escape from the hustle and bustle is not always easy. Recent news that attendance at UK visitor attractions is down 23 per cent on pre-pandemic levels highlighted the speed at which such sanctuaries are disappearing.

In the digital age, virtual third places initially seemed like a solution to the loss of physical ones. PlayStation borrowed the term 'The Third Place' for one of its most impactful early marketing blitzes. This was a smart move: games and social media used to be third places. Now they're second jobs. Social media is less a relaxed space for hanging out and more often about building a personal brand.

Play is vital to the development of children's minds and the well-being of adults. Sleep is essential to creativity, our ability to store memories and problem-solve. A good holiday renews our spirits. So it makes sense that there's a societal benefit to collective experiences that fulfil a similar function.

As our third places diminish, we must endeavour to create new ones. There's no place like a home from home.

— First published in March 2023 —

Spear's Awards 2022 acceptance speech

The Spear's Awards are held annually by the titular organisation to acknowledge the work of entrepreneurs, philanthropists and advisers to high-net-worth individuals. In 2022, Ajaz Ahmed was the recipient of the Impact Award "for his work with his foundation, Ajaz.org, and its support of disadvantaged families and children across the UK"

A mother dilutes her milk with water, so there's enough to feed her small children. A family shares bathwater because they can't afford to heat it.

A 10-year-old child asks if she can exchange the previously owned toy that she's just been handed for a bag of rice she's just spotted in the corner of the room, to make her mum happier at home.

These are not stories from a faraway and ancient land.

These are the truths from children and families in the UK today, the world's fifth-largest economy.

We live in a remarkable, inspiring country with a wealth of wisdom and treasured knowledge but sometimes a poverty of distribution. All too often, greater awareness does not equal greater understanding.

Sir Winston Churchill said, "We make a living by what we get. We make a life by what we give."

Everyone in this room is a trustee – a trustee for humanity and a trustee for our planet.

If the meaning of life is to discover your gift, then the purpose of life is to give it away. This award will encourage me to redouble our efforts for the many causes we are privileged to serve through ajaz.org

Thank you to Edwin and the Spears judges for this incredible recognition. I dedicate this honour to my phenomenal mother Sughran and my remarkable late father Khowaj who always gave the most but, at the time, had the least to give.

I would like to thank the wonderful Nicola Brentnall, my guide, for her significant depth of knowledge and expertise across the spectrum of issue areas we support. I would also like to thank the brilliant Sam Kelly and Raj Chaim for the extraordinary support they provide to me and our teams at AKQA every day.

Thank you.

The imitation game

We learn by watching others.
But we grow by thinking for ourselves

At school, copying was one of the few things the teacher and the cool kids agreed on. Whether you looked over a fellow student's shoulder to solve the maths problem or appeared one day with the same jacket or haircut as your hipper classmate, copycats were bad.

Looking back over the key news stories of summer 2024, it's easy to conclude that they had a point.

In Britain, fed a brazen lie by bad actors through their social media feeds, young people – many of them still in their teens, or younger – went on rampages through British cities in the name of 'justice'.

Across Europe, tourists endure misery, crowding and high prices to secure those perfect smiling holiday snaps – thus perpetuating the cycle of over-tourism, environmental degradation and aggrieved local populations.

Then, as the new school year approaches, Jonathan Haidt's screen-time warning *The Anxious Generation* becomes a bestseller and a key talking point among concerned modern parents, and a mobile network provider advises parents of younger children to buy them 'dumb' phones that will enable them to stay in contact, rather than 'smart' ones through which peer pressure and bad influencers might lead them astray.

In light of such stories, imitation starts to look like the severest form of flattening – of cultural diversity and of the ability of individuals to reason beyond the crude binaries of mob rule. Little wonder that the late philosopher René Girard's 'Mimetic Theory' has attracted such attention since the all-conquering ascent of social media, even though it's in many ways an origin story for the earliest days of human society.

Broadly speaking, Girard's argument is that, faced with the daunting prospect of choice and freedom to pursue our desires, we humans tend to copy the desires of others – either because we don't have our own, or we see the status value, the 'clout', in securing things that will make others envious. According to this theory, scapegoating is a structural inevitability of imitation: when countless people pursue a limited resource, an innocent and arbitrary 'other' must be ritually sacrificed to restore peace and dissipate envy. This seems especially timely – yet it can't be the whole story.

Having spent far too much of my recent screen time consumed by news about the hazards of imitation, the other day I opted for some soothing respite – David Attenborough's latest Netflix documentary. In *Secret Lives of Orangutans*, we meet Eden, an eight-year-old who, thanks to the arrival of a new baby in the family, must start fending for herself after a lifetime spent copying whatever her mother did. It's a reminder that imitation is an essential part of growing up.

Consider the famous painters whose early works ape their heroes, or literary critic Harold Bloom's theory of the 'Anxiety of Influence', which says literary greatness begins with the emulation of your idols, or the way your favourite band's early records often sound like their favourite bands – or the way we're all prone, in our teens, to trying on different personalities and styles and seeing what sticks.

So we can't eradicate the impulse to imitate – it goes back to the origin of our species, and its negative side effects show up in the earliest known human societies. For that reason, we should also avoid putting all the blame for the corrosive effects of modern copycatting on technology.

Yes, technology makes it very easy to jump on a bandwagon with one click. Yes, the structure of digital debate tends to drive us towards stubborn, binary ideological decisions. But no, it doesn't have to be that way.

We can use technology to help foster reflection instead of reaction. Look at the growing popularity of mind-mapping software, especially among neurodiverse people. It encourages people to join up their ideas and freely associate their thoughts to find their own way, instead of forcing them to fit into bullet points or binary, hashtagged opposites.

We can also make better use of technology so that young people looking for direction and meaning are neither censured for their curiosity nor drawn to online demagogues with easy answers. We don't hear about 'mentorship' as much as we used to, but it's a useful ideal when we think about how to better enable people to find their own voices and not get lost in the crowd.

From the reports of children starting school without the necessary social and language skills to the increasing reports of the expulsion of older kids, the long tail of the lockdown years is beginning to highlight the ways in which good guidance can be hard to find in our squeezed educational and community networks and the issues that arise when you delegate parenting to a smartphone.

In the absence of the human resources to help, AI, which is so often blamed for disseminating bad information, could be a valuable asset: screening out misinformation and providing useful context and verified data, anticipating the obvious ideological rabbit holes and scapegoats, and equipping people to think for themselves.

Serendipity
and learning

Unchained opportunity, the gift of liberty, a naive sense of immortality you have when you're 21 years old. The internet's perpetual promise of undiscovered terrain. These are the stars that aligned, the forces that collided to bring AKQA into existence – a seemingly impossible voyage seduced us, encouraging us to set sail.

Like all enduring stories, desire is at the heart of ours. And like any artistic endeavour, you make decisions from feeling, not reason. AKQA was founded with a yearning for textured work of passion and a sensitivity to evoke emotion. It is an ethos that holds the organisation together across studios and continents.

The cultural fabric that envelops AKQA and enables our values to thrive is the simple, notable sense of being a service provider that pushes the boundaries.

Service is one of our founding values and bestows the organisation with its soul and orientation, enabling it to stand the test of time. As the author of our values, I have always been inspired by the vibrancy and dynamism of nature and architecture. The organic unity of the living world, its magnetic allure, breathtaking magnificence, and enchantment of its all-encompassing systems conquers all. Nature is heartfelt; it lights up all the senses.

As with architecture, an intuitive, aesthetic perspective permeates through the work and shapes the company. AKQA is designed to be an organisation that has endurance, courage and an open mind. An optimistic mindset rooted in adaptability that – despite the world's unrelenting mutability – enables us to look ahead, do the things that might never have been done before, recover from difficulties and sustain beyond any individual.

How do you design an organisation to have courage? It's about instilling a freedom to experiment and an understanding that everything can evolve – that 'mistakes' are a natural part of the learning process. If we fear getting it wrong, we fear taking risks, and if we can't subvert, then we can't pioneer. Innovation is by its nature an experiment with uncertain outcomes. The research from this curiosity provides better judgement, which leads to new possibilities.

Everyone who shares our journey is hopefully inspired by the dreams that emerge from an imaginative application of art and science to create memorable work of resonance. It should speak a language that has universal appeal and makes an impact of no small magnitude. Ultimately, we are problem solvers.

If the defining characteristics of AKQA's philosophy are creative experimentation and pushing the limits, then there are also consistent themes within it: the belief that stories told through software can be vivid and captivating, that technology can create empathy and that a different perspective elevates the spirit.

The work should speak for itself. It shouldn't need any sense of salesmanship or embellishment. It's about avoiding complacency to find the next creative challenge. That's also why breaking the mould and new horizons motivate us. It's why the future is the place that occupies most of our thoughts and activities.

Underpinning this work is the repertoire of vision, beliefs, attitudes, practices and stories represented in our culture. All organisations are an innate reflection of the behaviours of their people, the interconnectivity and unique manifestation of influences, motivations, relationships and serendipity have occurred on their journey, together and apart. Every action and interaction adds a new dimension even if we're not conscious of it at the time.

The bravery that's articulated in the willingness to explore new solutions in our work is the same spirit that fuels the organisation's geographic footprint and aspirations of the team. You don't grow from astonishingly humble origins, where the odds were not in our favour, to 2,000 people collaborating across 23 international cities, without courage.

While you explore cities, you learn about their apparent contradictions. San Francisco has the highest average family income of any major metropolis in the States and is famously home to many industrious billionaires who have created extraordinary inventions, yet there are estimates of 7,000–20,000 homeless people on its streets. Tokyo is one of the world's fastest, most crowded and busiest cities. It is also one of the most organised, peaceful and tranquil. The world's most populous city is the least violent. For centuries, London has been a mosaic of the exotic and the embodiment of ethnic and cultural diversity, where around a third of inhabitants are born overseas, yet for years, Brexit was the dominant conversation, dividing families as well as communities.

All countries are at their greatest when the better angels of our nature are revealed through fairness, respect, and intellect. When prosperous people help all to prosper, everyone benefits.

My motivations have always come from a place of service, no matter what. To remain relevant and beneficial, we need to cooperate and make ourselves useful. The ingredients of successful cooperation are conveyed through compassion, empathy and understanding.

When I think about my happiest times, they've unquestionably arisen when I've been in service personally, or when, collectively, our team has created an enticing idea that's of use and inspiration. The best reward is when audiences respond to the work. That's the highlight of any career.

The natural progression of this idea of service is that there is going to come a time in the not-too-distant future when I dedicate a vast amount of my time to not-for-profit endeavours. Over the past decade, I've spent a fair amount of time with charitable organisations, both as a supporter and a student. I've learned about the unsung heroes whose rays of light awaken our better angels. Their nobility of spirit and tremendous capacity for understanding, humility and absence of ego help to positively transform lives but also inherently modify the way we view the world.

You can't just walk away from a feeling as strong as this. You can't sleep peacefully when you've encountered hardships and degradation. Maybe it's because I didn't grow up in a city but connected to nature. Perhaps it's my parents' example of kindness and generosity that knows no bounds. Most likely, it's the shoulders of giants I've had the fortune to stand on and to learn from and see the positive difference they've made.

We all grow and change throughout our lives as we learn that no life is all plain sailing. We understand the value of loss in a world that's built for winners. The storms of disappointment and difficulty, tribulation and adversity catch us by surprise – but they pass. We should never lose hope. What we all hope for is a peaceful world that's full of good vibes, free of discord and devastation. For this to happen, a new conversation has to emerge that's more about community and collaboration and less about conflict and competition.

It's an idealistic view, but surely if you're a media owner or a tech firm, you not only want to educate the public but you want to help them to be wise. Perhaps we should reconsider our definitions of success. Instead of the relentless obsession with economic growth, could organisations be measured by their positive contribution to society and well-being for our planet? We know that wildlife is a public good that must be protected, so couldn't we calculate the cost of our environmental damage and pay back the biological preservation and enhancement bill that Mother Nature never sends us? These thoughts may be imperfect, but none of us can ignore the challenge of seeking better solutions.

Creativity, ideas and the imagination have the power to break down barriers, bring people together and shape a more harmonious future for all. Word of mouth is still the most influential medium. Stories will forever be the most profound catalysts of change.

Our era's great tragedy is also its most significant opportunity: the vast wealth of resources in severe contrast with the poverty of sharing them.

We have witnessed and experienced extraordinary, hopeful technological and social change in our lifetimes. If humans are the primary cause of conflict and destruction, then we can also be the facilitators of healing and renewal.

— First published in Semi-Permanent *in May 2018 —*

Nature

We do not inherit the Earth from our ancestors; we borrow it from our children

First, the bad news. First, because our ability to avoid facing the bad news is half the problem. Bad, because if we look at the crises facing the natural world in standard human terms of success and failure, it's already over. The winners are humans, the losers are everything else. The statistical trends for the loss of species and habitats are so stark that no numerate adult would reasonably expect them to stop plummeting until they hit zero.

We've lost 70 per cent of the planet's vertebrates since 1970 and more than half of its marine life. Our food adulterants and our medicines are over-dosing many remaining sea creatures with estrogens at pollutant levels, per-turbing fish physiology and affecting reproductive development in animals – and they are also linked with breast cancer in women and prostate cancer in men. The world's population of insects, so vital as food for other animals and pollinators for humans, is 25 per cent of what it was three decades ago. World-renowned natural habitats are suffering and shrinking faster than ever – rainforests are being razed from Australia to Brazil. Deforestation for ag-riculture, overgrazing and the use of agrochemicals has resulted in dramatic degradation of soil, leading to pollution, flooding and desertification. Once fertile land transformed into desert through loss of vegetation, water and wildlife spurs human displacement. At the local and national level, we're los-ing animals that have long been fixtures in national folk culture. In the UK, hedgehogs are among the many small mammals disappearing along with the environment that supported them, and the population of nightingales has de-clined by 91 per cent in 40 years, with the threat of development looming over several of their remaining nesting sites.

It seems silly to talk about good news in the face of such staggering statis-tics, but it is vital to do just that if we're to do anything about the trends they convey. The first glimmer of good news is that things have gotten so bad that we find ourselves at a moment of opportunity. There's nothing left to waste energy on arguing about and no remaining gains to be had from pointing fingers. You don't even have to believe in human-made global warming to feel the impact of rising seas, ever-hotter summers and more widespread and resilient wildfires. You don't have to care about the bees to care that a third of humanity's crop yield is dependent on their work.

The second shred of good news is that, right now, there is still enough nature around for us to observe, enjoy and learn from. If we make a little bit of an effort and forego the little bit of box-set time it takes to do that, we can witness how fruitless and strangely human it is to settle either for giving up or feeling angry. With its cycles of decline and renewal, its transformations of waste into nourishment and new life, and its ability to turn every ending into a new beginning, the natural world reminds us how wasteful and simplistic our focus on short-term triumph tends to be. When there's a shaft of sunlight or a puddle of rainwater in a roadside ditch, nature never says no to even the flimsiest opportunity to bring new life into the world.

Nature's systems of recovery and resurrection will continue to surprise us, for the simple reason that, though we know a great deal, all humankind's understanding still amounts to a partial, crude comprehension of systems and species. We're only just learning how to slow down birdsong so its melodic craft is evident to the human ear and beginning to get a handle on the particular intelligence of octopuses, armed with 10,000 more genes than humans. Elsewhere, we're still making breathtaking discoveries about nature's ingenious routes to resilience. Sometimes, it takes a seeming disaster to show even the experts that their worst fears are unfounded. The South East of England, where I grew up, generally gets it easy in the world table of natural disasters, which is why it was such a shock to leave for school one October morning in 1987 and realise, as I walked, that the 120mph winds of the previous night's Great Storm had pulled down brick walls, bent metal bus shelters and felled trees that I'd known all my life. Later, I heard how many lives had been lost, but first thing that morning, there was a *Wizard of Oz* wonder to it all, not to mention the sudden possibility of a day off school in it for me. But that morning's shock wasn't tempered by any such treats for the staff at Kew's Royal Botanical Garden. Most had got to work by the early hours that morning to assess the damage, which was colossal. Kew's world-famous arboretum had been devastated by the winds, and many of its oldest and rarest trees had been lost. In the days and weeks that followed, as the damage was methodically surveyed and discussions began about replacing what had gone, the despair only darkened. The arboretum had been the reference point for their work for centuries, and now it was largely flattened. Beyond it, there was no known authoritative guide to undertaking such a major project, no agreed-upon library or book of proven information about how to replace such precious trees. It seemed that what they'd lost might well prove irreplaceable.

On the brink of despair but unwilling to abandon hope, Kew's staff reached out to botanical gardens, nurseries and amateur enthusiasts worldwide, asking for any specimens, information or observations about the exotic varieties they had lost and the care of trees in general. As replies began to come in, those Kew staff realised that, all around the world, people had been doing research, dutifully taking cuttings, noting surprising details about the ways trees worked. By collating all this disparate knowledge and organising the newly arrived specimens gifted by strangers, Kew's staff effectively ended up compiling the 'Tree Bible' they wished had existed on that mid-October morning after. They realised that established rules of tree care they had obeyed for years were wrong – so, for example, it turned out that tying saplings to stakes to give them support prevented them from developing the resilience they needed to thrive as adult trees. A greater shock still was another discovery that flew in the face of gardening wisdom: they discovered that roots grow out from, rather than underneath, trees. Very few species have roots that ever get more than a metre below the ground. The fate of one particular tree embodied this welcome revelation.

It was known as the 'Turner Oak', and it and its roots had been seen to come right out of the ground during the storm. When the clear-up began, the fact that it had been ripped from the ground meant that the Turner Oak was assumed doomed and tagged for removal. But because the workload with less hopeless cases was so great, it took three years for Kew staff to get to the Turner Oak. By the time they did, they saw, with amazement, that the oak was already recovering. Its moment of levitation had not doomed it but reinvigorated it. Because it was lifted from the soil, long compacted by the feet of thousands of visitors to Kew, oxygen had finally reached its roots. By 1992, the Turner Oak was a third larger than it had been before the hurricane. Five years after the Great Storm had seemingly sentenced it to death, it had grown more than it had in the previous several decades.

Since 1987, for all we've lost of the natural world, we've made more such miraculous discoveries. The one-time logger and now bestselling, tree-hugging author Peter Wohlleben, has written about trees that sprout leaves five years after falling, presumed dead. Others are still unpacking the intricate, unseen ways in which tree roots and fungi communicate underground or how they chemically warn each other of threats above them. The natural world is still yielding secrets that show us how petty and impatient our understanding of defeat and victory is – but the time we have left to learn from them is limited.

There will be more such amazing discoveries even while the clock ticks and more uplifting and inspiring surprises. If we're to do them justice, to learn from them and to apply nature's wisdom to human affairs, we have to be harder on some of our own ideas.

Like those Kew tree people, we have to be willing to re-examine standard wisdom when it proves destructive. For example, our definition of economic 'growth', tied up as it is with cheap oil, deforestation, construction and the rest, with international competition rather than collaboration, is a strangely 20th-century one. Immediately after the 2008 financial crash, voices were heard asking whether we didn't need a more subtle metric, a sense of 'growth' and progress that didn't rest on the loss and deterioration of the natural world and the soil, air and water on which we all depend. These voices are too rarely heard today, but they are still there – the economists pointing out how old-fashioned and cripplingly short-termist our sense of wealth and national well-being is; the tree lovers reminding leaf-averse planners that, with its effect on air quality and house prices, a tree on a residential street not only provides a home to 1,000 living things but also adds a value of over $10,000 in cold, hard cash.

Beyond that, we don't need clever economists; we just need a willingness to stop to consider what we're doing and what it means for the world we'll grow old in, the world we'll pass on to our children. We also need to ask whether they'll be able to forgive us if we don't. Policy-makers and powerful people do occasionally get animated about these looming issues – but rarely and fleetingly. Late in 2017, British MPs briefly became vocal about the amount of plastic in our oceans (and in fish and ultimately in us), but that was only after a screening of the ominous final episode of Sir David Attenborough's *Blue Planet II*. Whales, dolphins, sharks, fish, birds, sea turtles, citizens who've listened to Dame Ellen MacArthur or school kids who've visited aquariums have been worrying about it for years. This isn't news out there in the real world.

A little over 50 years ago, the great American author and illustrator Theodore Geisel – aka Dr Seuss – published a book called *The Lorax*, about what would happen if humans kept plundering nature without a thought for what the world would be like once they'd got rich off its resources. On its heartbreaking final page, a rich, miserly, lonely old man throws the last fertile seed to a young boy and asks him to plant it – to do a better job as steward of the world's living things than his generation has. As someone born a few years after *The Lorax*, I can put my hand up and say we've failed emphatically at that. But that doesn't mean that the book's urgent instruction to do something, rather than carry on doing what we're doing, has lost any of its relevance.

After reading *Sapiens* by Yuval Noah Harari, I was left with the thought perhaps Homo sapiens will not cease the path of menace and destruction until alas there is nothing left to ruin. Commentators talk of "the end of the world". I see it differently. Humans represent just 0.01 per cent of all life but have destroyed 83 per cent of wild mammals. In our disrespect for the species we share this planet with, humans are destroying themselves. The natural world is collateral damage until the point where humans have meandered into our own extinction, and it is able to thrive once again.

It's customary for warm-hearted people to sincerely say, if asked how they'd like to be remembered, that they'd like to leave the world a slightly better place. When we look at those plummeting statistics from the natural world with which we began, it becomes clear that this is, by many measures, an impossible aim. On the other hand, provided we're still paying attention to nature, we know that we can still make the effort to make even the smallest acts, and that those efforts will all have consequences.

While there's still a seed to send out on the wind, still a crack of earth in the paving for it to fall in, nature won't stop trying to renew itself. And whatever angst or powerlessness we feel about the policies of our government or the airborne toxins outside our front doors, we can all make the world a slightly greener place. We can do it in the most literal, simple ways, and we can make it a slightly more hospitable home to all life in the process.

— First published in Defeat *in 2019 —*

The future past

Invited recently to name his favourite ever war movies, the military historian Antony Beevor chose *The Battle of Algiers* and *The 317th Platoon*. Those two films, long revered by cineastes for their technique, were also commended by Beevor for their fidelity to known historical fact. Having been an expert adviser on several high-profile 'based on a true story' films of recent years and a careful viewer of scores more, he clearly came at the question of war films from a position of some authority. Yet both of his selections were first released over half a century ago – something Beevor saw less as a triumph of the past and more as an indictment of the present.

Of course, Hollywood has never been a place to allow historical accuracy to get in the way of a good story. But from Beevor's insider perspective, the industry's need for black-and-white morality, heroes, villains and happy endings has, during the past 20 years, led to more shameless and drastic rewriting of history than before. Over the same period, he argued, as our culture has become ever more visual, we've had less contact with other sources for our ideas about history, so the movie versions dominate our attempts to imagine it. As Beevor knows, we're all complicit in this process, expecting edifying, uplifting historical 'experiences' but keen to avoid nagging ambiguities and too-awful realities: "People are more likely to want to see something they think is very close to the truth, so they can feel they are learning as well as being entertained. In a post-literate society, the moving image is king, and most people's knowledge of history is regrettably based more on cinematic fiction than archival fact."

In this latest year of important anniversaries, it seems self-evident that our culture is obsessed with history. The march of big-money streaming TV means there are more hours of opulent historical drama on our screens than ever before. Pivotal past events are freely invoked by politicians and pundits claiming to see into the future. Humble symbols of remembrance are the subjects of grand displays and annual media furores. History is even something you get to walk through, thanks to VR headsets or ancient Egyptian tourist modes in hit video games like *Assassin's Creed*.

On closer inspection, though, many of those other contemporary experiences of history seem closer to Beevor's modern Hollywood model than we'd like to admit. Those expensive TV dramas are packed with beautiful people whose grooming and dialogue are tailored to our times, not theirs. The theatre revivals that sell out and make headlines are the ones that rework classics in accordance with modern mores. Though they are useful tools, those digital trips to real historical epochs can also give us the illusion of being able to summon the past at the tap of a screen or a nod of the head. A contested and sketchy scene from the past can become a vivid virtual reality. The lure of interactivity can end up distracting us from the mental effort of imagining life in another era. Even academic TV historians now routinely talk about the partially recovered past in the definitive present tense, with the same objective of engaging and immersing us in it. We all love the pomp, but few of us have patience for the nuances of real historical circumstance.

If we're only seeing the 'history' we want, like people watching a YouTube channel of '80s pop videos that never were, it doesn't matter how much of it we consume. If our favoured forms of history merely reflect the desires of today back at us, they can't help us understand our lives yesterday or tomorrow.

The summer of 2019 witnessed the passing of 30 years since the publication of political scientist Francis Fukuyama's famous essay 'The End of History'. Published as the Eastern Bloc crumbled in 1989, Fukuyama's essay was first celebrated as the herald of a new era of peaceful, global capitalism under a single guiding superpower. Fifteen years later, in the wake of the wars, terror and geopolitical shifts of the early 21st century, 'The End of History' was frequently portrayed as an awfully premature, thoroughly hubristic idea.

Today, the downbeat conclusion to Fukuyama's upbeat essay is what resonates: "The end of history will be a very sad time. The struggle for recognition, the willingness to risk one's life for a purely abstract goal, the worldwide ideological struggle that called forth daring, courage, imagination, and idealism, will be replaced by economic calculation, the endless solving of technical problems, environmental concerns, and the satisfaction of sophisticated consumer demands… there will be neither art nor philosophy, just the perpetual caretaking of the museum of human history. I can feel in myself, and see in others around me, a powerful nostalgia for the time when history existed."

'History' is everywhere in our 21st-century museum – but because we whitewash the walls, sweep the dirt under the carpets and wallow in the warmth of retro references, it is a very particular, selective sort.

There are many histories available to us – and the vast amount of information available on the internet and the live responses to current events on social media have helped demonstrate that there's no such thing as impartial reporting of the news.

We need to get used to hearing more than one version of events and using our judgement to decide what we think is fake news. If people were more educated on the horrors of empire or the wars and persecution caused around the world, they might be less susceptible to implicit racial bias in the media as well as in retellings of history. They might be more sceptical about what they see as trusted sources and more open to other accounts.

Our relationship with the future is strikingly similar: we're comfortable with simple, broad-brush statements about salvation via technology or destruction through environmental ruin, but when it comes to the stark detail, we're all terrible at facing up to the data.

Over the past couple of years, with much of the world's English-speaking media focused on a pair of unexpected electoral outcomes, scores of significant, peer-reviewed studies carrying stark statistical warnings about looming disasters have come and gone from the headlines. A third of the Great Barrier Reef is dead and will never return. The world's population of vertebrates has shrunk by 70 per cent in under half a century. Its insect population has declined by 75 per cent in three decades, with airborne insects now disappearing at a rate of 6 per cent per year. Marine life and seabird populations are being razed by overfishing, pollution and warming seas. A young whale died with 88 pounds of plastic in its stomach while a plastic bag was found over 10,000 metres below sea level in the Mariana Trench, grimly expressing the depth of our problem.

Once upon a time, we might have foolishly told ourselves that the sufferings of other species were a sad but unavoidable cost of human progress. Today, such fables seem simplistic or even absurd – not only because our 'progress' as a species is complicated by the growing wealth gap, anger and narcissism fed by our news and social media bubbles, but also because we can no longer pretend that changes in the natural world don't have consequences for the human one.

A leaked report that the US Food and Drug Administration declined to publish last year tested a wide variety of fruit, grains and vegetables; not one was without traces of a pesticide studies have linked to cancer. Besides that, the demands of consumers, retailers and agriculture mean that the fruit and vegetables we eat are becoming progressively less nutritious. It's not only the world's soil where fertility is in steep decline; male sperm counts have halved in the past 40 years, too.

Carlo Rovelli, the latest physicist to translate mind-boggling concepts into a popular bestseller, writes, "The difference between past and future, between cause and effect, between memory and hope, between regret and intention… in the elementary laws that describe the mechanism of the world, there is no such difference."

That might sound like cosmic boffin-speak, far removed from the real world. But in our 21st century, as MRI technology has transformed research into the brain, neuroimaging has shown that the nature of brain activation for both episodic memory and imagining the future is almost impossible to distinguish, with the hippocampus working the same way for each.

This discovery has led to a tenfold increase in research on the connection between memory and imagination. Our brains know that our ability to face the future rests on our willingness to engage with the past, even if we don't.

Faced with the kind of shocking statistics that are now a daily event, we need to get beyond feeling helpless and dispirited. We need to avoid laying all the blame on enemies and resist the urge to retreat into our safe spaces. And the heartening news is that, outside the pressured, short-termist worlds of politics and the media, there are people who might point the way to remind us that there are different, potentially more productive ways to engage with what is past and what is yet to come.

Jorie Graham, one of America's most garlanded living poets, has spoken recently of the need to think differently about our future. She argues that scary statistics or warnings from scientists aren't enough to make us rethink our relationship with the future – our own imagination is vital, too. Graham says that our digital-era preoccupation with a 'perpetual present' of alerts and distractions and the outsourcing of memory to technology means we struggle to engage with the 'deep past' and thus the 'deep future.' Only imagination will enable us to care for future generations.

We can't wish the future away or close our eyes until it looks the way we want it to. But we can at least try to make it more welcoming for humans and other living things. There's no better, more empowering motivation than the knowledge that we should, and could, be doing a whole lot better.

— Originally published in Defeat *in 2019 —*

What we
show
and
do
is more
important
than what
we say.

CULTURE IS NOT WHAT YOU PREACH.

IT'S WHAT YOUR DECISIONS PROTECT.

The small things

say the
big things.

THE SIMPLE WILL ALWAYS DISPLACE THE COMPLEX

Creativity

is an

optimistic
act.

What *we* create in the world builds *us.*

Reputation and trust are more important than growth.

CLIENTS HIRE US BECAUSE WE ARE AN ENERGY,

NOT BECAUSE
WE ARE AN
AGENCY

When you give
away an idea
you make room
for another.

Win without
boasting.
Lose without
moaning.

The concept of quality is difficult to define for it is not merely seen but somehow intuited in the presence of the work in which it is embodied.

4

Origins & Inspirations

Start-ups are the vital new blood of business. But they'd be nothing without the wisdom of those who paved the way

The way I see it

This article originated as a series of interview questions by Shots *magazine and was first published in its October 2016 issue*

I was born at the Canadian Red Cross Hospital in Taplow, a village in Buckinghamshire, England, that sits on the River Thames.

My earliest memory is my mother peeling and deseeding a pomegranate for us to eat.

Both my parents worked remarkably hard. My father has a zen, meditative calm about him, and my mum is a force of nature: restless, very energetic. My mother worked in the local hospital and my dad as a machinist in a local factory. We didn't grow up with much, but what they did give me is the best gift: a limitless love of learning and liberty.

My childhood was wonderful. I grew up in a big family surrounded by nature, sunshine and freedom, which was paradise for me. As a teenager, I went sailing most weekends, and in those moments, the sea cast its endlessly seductive spell on me, creating many of my life's happiest memories. It was idyllic. Nature makes all the senses light up: sight, touch, smell, sound and taste. Digital is not truly multisensory in the way that nature is, not even close. My memorable moments with nature are engraved into my heart. I can't say that about digital experiences yet, but it will happen.

I've always loved reading, so as a child, the idea of becoming a writer had an appeal.

At school, I probably asked too many questions because I'm curious about examining the roots of things and the way things work. But if it was a choice between being a good student or being able to enjoy my life at school, then I chose the latter option. There's no rule that says you need to be at school to be a good student because the desire to learn never actually stops.

There are so many subjects I'm interested in, but what got me into technology and communications in the first place was architecture. I fell in love with a building. I grew up in the Thames Valley, essentially the Silicon Valley of the UK. There were technology companies sprouting up all over the place. Most workplaces were anonymous office blocks that lacked soul, but there was one perfect building that I used to walk past almost every day on my paper round when I was 12 years old. I wanted to know everything about the company that occupied it, what kind of work they did and what the people in it were like.

I went on to learn that they were the world's largest database software company. They had about 80 per cent market share at one point. When you think that almost all the digital services we use these days are databases of some kind, this company could have been one of the most powerful in the world if it were still around today.

I wrote one letter after another to try and to get a job with them. Then one day, after I had written my 11th letter, an envelope arrived at my parents' house. The lady who delivered it looked like an angel to me! The letter said that as soon as I had a national insurance number, I could work for them. That year I got my national insurance number, and they employed me for a week. A week turned into a few years, working after school and during holidays. I loved it. They had me work in every department: development, logistics, distribution, finance, marketing, sales, operations and training – everywhere. I learned such a massive amount.

At university in Bath, I lived on campus with two friends who also had four names, so we would playfully refer to one another using our initials rather than forenames. It's a very 'university' thing to do. (My full name is Ajaz Khowaj Quoram Ahmed. Khowaj is the name of my father and grandfather.)

In the same way that I knew if I didn't go to university I would regret it, I also knew if I didn't leave university to start AKQA, then I would have regretted that too. By the time I got to university I had already been working for about six years. In that time, I had learned a lot about the standards that the best companies have. I won't ever encourage anyone to drop out of university, but I do encourage people to never lose their curiosity. I enjoyed my time at university because I met people who have become friends for life, and AKQA still has an association with the university today. We hire a lot of people from Bath University because it's a wonderful place that attracts good people.

There's no question that while I was growing up, every adult I met was a mentor of one kind or another – there were so many saints in my life. Today, we hire people for what they can teach us and not just what we can teach them. Over the years, I've been tremendously lucky to have worked with or learned from remarkable people.

'Welcome to the fast lane!' was my attitude to work in the early days of my career. There's always been restlessness, and even as I've grown, it has not been diluted. If anything, it has accelerated.

At AKQA, we are so fortunate to work with progressive clients around the world that share our values and perspectives, creating a ripple effect that extends far beyond any of our own organisations. Virgin has been with us since the beginning, when a project I designed and programmed as a youngster caught its attention. They invited me in for a meeting, and we just clicked.

The shared values, the enthusiasm, fun and the love of creativity made a strong connection, and it has strengthened ever since.

I'm always going to be grateful to Nike for the journey so far and the adventures ahead. There really isn't a company on earth like Nike. It's in a category of one. We've learned so much working together. In the early days, we were approached by staff from one of their competitors, who offered us an extraordinary amount of money to start working with them instead. We turned the offer down politely and told them: "Nike isn't just another client, it's a part of our soul."

What sets AKQA apart is we've never lost our ability to surprise. All our best ideas can be explained in one line. They have a sense of humanity and universality to them. Our work is the imaginative application of art and science. We know we are not in the business of creating technology, but we are in the business of applying it in an exciting way. That's why we say that the most powerful force in the universe isn't technology, it's imagination.

How would I define innovation? Well, they say "Today's innovation is tomorrow's tradition". And there's a quote by William Gibson: "The future is already here – it's just not very evenly distributed". So I think of AKQA being in the 'evenly distributing the future' business.

You have to stay hungry, otherwise you go stale. AKQA is about the duality of what may first appear to be opposing forces. We're about pushing the limits and explorations, counterbalanced with good engineering and execution. We're about youth and energy, counterbalanced with maturity and experience. We're about the cutting-edge, the state of the art, but we've never forgotten our origins. We're about creating what's next, but nostalgic and loyal too.

This means we're open to drawing upon outside influences beyond the narrow confines of one industry. We're always searching for sensory material that can challenge us in new ways. But although the pillars and foundations of our company are firm, we're adaptive and sensitive to changes in the business environment and society.

Two truths have given us a head start. The first is that technology will shape culture. The second is the need for professionals to help organisations navigate this landscape in the best way, so the productivity of their investments is amplified.

The advice I'd give anyone seeking to enter this business is that you need to be vibrant and resilient. If you can't tolerate the honest feedback it takes to make the work better, and if you can't suffer failures and setbacks, then this business is not for you. From our early days, we've aimed to hire as many fascinating, eccentric, abnormal and unusual misfits as we can.

The advertising industry is fighting a perpetual battle against its own obsolescence. Most of the work produced is destined for the scrap heap, which makes for inconvenient knowledge. If the ad business is rooted in creativity, then why are most ads disposable and dull? How many commercials are a revelation and leave the screen with you?

Most ads are like fast food. You eat it, and a few minutes later you're hungry again. If you do it too much, it will numb your mind.

The problem with a lot of advertising is simply that the sum is less than the parts. It's become too much about the copy and not enough about the feeling: that's just lazy. If the words were any good, then it would be more bearable, but there's an abundance of clichés. We live in a world of images, but there are more words than ever. Given the visual sophistication of international audiences, you'd think the industry would try harder to raise its head above the parapet and avoid just going through the motions.

Then there's the predictability. Take the 'manifesto film' that's so popular at the moment – usually a voiceover set to a montage of feelgood images tuned to a trite rendition of a long-forgotten song. Audiences filter out this self-righteous 'talking to itself' nonsense. Good work carves a crevice in your synapses, it stays with you.

The conventional picture of entrepreneurs as 'one-person-wonders' is a romantic one. We need a hero behind the events we witness to help make sense of them, but the reality is more complicated. We need to get away from the narcissism that comes from propagating the idea that the progress of an organisation can be down to just one person. It's not about being an auteur. It's about the humility to accept that everything we do is an ensemble piece.

You can read as many books about leadership as you like, but it basically boils down to one thing: be a decent human being. There's a straightforward course in management for anyone who wants to be better and it goes along the lines of: make a short list of all the things that have been done to you that annoyed you. And never do them to others. Then make a list of the things done to you that you've loved. And do those always. I think business is not about complexity but about simple philosophies that anyone can understand. That's what really resonates.

My first book *Velocity* was published in 2012 and has been the gift that's not stopped giving. People used to know me as the founder of AKQA, but now I often hear, "Oh, you're the guy who wrote *Velocity*." Then they tell me about the impact that the book has had on their life and the way they think about business. It was written for entrepreneurs and businesses, but a lot of feedback I get is from not-for-profits and community organisations implementing the thinking and getting results. That's rewarding.

My co-author Stefan Olander, Nike's head of digital sport, and I had been talking about writing a book for some time, but with demanding day jobs and families, it was tough to dedicate the time a project like this needs. It was the combination of the financial crisis in 2008 and the 2011 London riots that really spurred us on to complete the book.

We started AKQA in a recession and I wasn't exactly born with a silver spoon in my mouth, so I suppose *Velocity* was a humble reminder that, with the right motivation, you can help create jobs in a world of business turmoil. The thought was that if this book inspires a single company to keep investing or helps an entrepreneur to start something, then that's mission accomplished.

Shortly after finishing the book, I came across some pretty remarkable figures about the absence of longevity in business today: 87 per cent of companies in the Fortune 500 in 1955 no longer existed in 2011. The 500 most valuable companies in the USA today will only have a lifespan of 18 years. In 1958, that lifespan was around 61 years. For start-ups, it's even more accelerated: 71 per cent are gone within 10 years, while 55 per cent disappear within three years. But we all know there are companies that have existed for decades. So I was curious to discover if there was a philosophy common to those organisations that I could learn and share.

In that respect, my second book *Limitless* was more of a personal project, paying respect to the organisations and people that have meant something to me by telling the stories of leaders who, with an egalitarian vision, invite the chance of creating real change by giving to the many what is held by the few. But the learnings from it are universal, namely that the most transformative organisations and teams aren't the ones whose leaders shout the loudest.

The last book in the trilogy, called *Defeat,* will be out in 2019. And then I'm done with writing for a bit.

My dad doesn't talk much, but when he does, he usually has a proverb or some wisdom to share. The best piece of advice he ever gave me was, basically, not to sell your soul. If you lose money, you always have the opportunity to make it again, but with the others once they're gone, they're gone.

In the beginning and the end, what matters is the results. Is our work effective and enjoyed? Creative merit and commercial success are just two sides of the same coin. Brands that vault past their competitors are the ones that have purpose at the core, creativity in their veins and a strong sense of identity.

Whenever I've done a personality test, it always says I'm an introvert, but I think most people, including me, fall somewhere in the middle of being an introvert or an extrovert. We all recharge our brains through sleep. When we're with interesting people or being stimulated through learning or trying new things, we get energised, and when we're not, our energy gets depleted.

I've never done a digital detox. In my job, I don't think it's the responsible course of action not to be connected. But the way that I use technology is that it is of service to me rather than the other way around. I'm not particularly organised with my life outside of work and there have been so many occasions where my phone has proactively helped me get somewhere on time or given me health advice just because an algorithm recognised its importance in my life. When the technology is an agent of sorts, then that's the ultimate detox because it takes the pressure off.

My hobbies are swimming, reading and movies. In addition to family, friends and work, these are my greatest sources of pleasure. My happiest days involve sport or being with family and friends. I've not been sailing since I was a teenager and I'm saving it up so when I go I can really enjoy it.

The greatest human invention is probably the compass or inventions related to healthcare, medicine and improving people's lives. The worst are the ones that harm the lives of people or species we share this planet with. But you don't want to be part of the problem, you want to be part of the solution. As Leonardo da Vinci said, "Human subtlety will never devise an invention more beautiful, more simple or more direct than does nature because in her inventions nothing is lacking, and nothing is superfluous." Nothing is lacking, and nothing is superfluous – I think that's the ultimate aspiration.

I'm an optimist and an idealist, so if I were UK Prime Minister for the day, I would champion the idea that world peace is both possible and inevitable. I would make it our government's single most pressing priority to help create world peace with all nations in the smartest, most intelligent and nonviolent way. And that's mostly about education.

With the combined forces of knowledge, technology and wealth that the world has access to today – an abundance that's unprecedented in history – I really believe we can create more progress in the next few decades than we have in the past 200 years. Considered collectively, the world has an unlimited amount of knowledge and resources: hopefully, it will lead to more meaningful and enjoyable lives for everyone too.

The older I get, the more I learn how little I know. But if I am remembered then it should be for being a man who had nothing left to give. I love this quote from Robert Frost: "In three words I can sum up everything I've learned about life: it goes on."

The spirit is strong, but the body is tired

In memory of my dad, Khowaj Ahmed

5 JULY 1938 — 16 OCTOBER 2016

"Men like my father cannot die. They are with me still, real in memory as they were in flesh, loving and beloved forever…"

Monday was the first day in two weeks I had not been at my father's bedside. Instead, I joined him on our final journey together – to the grave where his body was laid to rest.

A couple of weeks prior, I had spent each day at the hospital observing the screen with his vital signs more keenly than a competitive trader might their Bloomberg terminal.

A few days in, when he wasn't unconscious, I managed to have a brief, albeit one-way, conversation. After his heart stopped beating on the morning of 2 October, he had a breathing tube inflating his lungs and all sorts of other apparatus doing the work his body no longer could. I asked if he was in pain. With a slight head gesture, he signalled "no".

I reminded him of the time I was born. The country was in recession and our family, like many families, had trouble making ends meet. My parents were now distant and destitute of a bountiful farm, mango orchards and a generous community that nourished them in a previous era and instead found themselves exhausted and alone.

Though my grandfather had served in the British Army, my parents were unaware they could claim welfare, raising a family of four (five with my arrival), on a factory worker's meagre salary.

The hardship was so severe that my dad had been warned bailiffs were to mercilessly confiscate the few possessions in the single room our family occupied in a communal house. There was little for the bailiffs to take, but there was the additional threat of daunting legal ramifications. His response to this burden: "…I don't mind. God just gave me a diamond." I held his hand and said, "When I was born, you said I was a diamond. Well, you're my diamond."

Lying flat in his bed, kept alive by wires, drips and tubes everywhere in his body, he lifted my hand as far as he could, twice, and tilted his head towards me. I saw a glimmer in his eyes. Overflowing with gratitude, at that moment, every appetite within me was satisfied. Even now – after everything he has been through – Dad is giving us his all.

Being in the hospital's intensive care unit for two weeks, I was constantly reminded of the sadness and joys of existence. Not a day goes by when there are not floods of tears as someone new is admitted. Nearly every day, someone dies or is about to. Many of the families never manage to have any final moments with the people who matter most to them. Even though it was only two weeks, I became an old-timer there. I got to know the regulars (like me) and the new arrivals. I introduced visitors of different backgrounds and cultures, so we could know one another through this – surely the most grim and testing of tribulations.

I did what I could to provide comfort and encouragement, to not lose hope when families thought the worst. Other times I would just listen, share food, offer a smile and a hug.

I overheard a tearful lady called Jane on her phone (her mother thankfully made a recovery). Jane was speaking compassionately about refugees and what she had seen. I hurried after her and we talked. I was able to assist the charities her church is connected with to make life more bearable for people who suffer extraordinary hardship and pain, with little respite, week in and week out.

One of the many lessons I have learned over the past few weeks is this: we are the lucky ones. We have safe hospitals and kind people. We live in countries where people are able to respect life, one another and the laws of the land.

My dad has now left this land. No more medicines. No more operations. No more needles, drips, insertions or extractions. There are no more hospitals where – despite the visits and the busyness – he was alone, away from the people, home and books he loved. There is no more pain to endure and no more pretending everything is OK because he doesn't want to put anyone out.

Born in India in 1938, my dad was a serene and decent man who was devoted to, and honoured, our mother. He loved his family of four children and five grandchildren. A descendant of the Chauhan clan, he carried with him the virtues of his lineage. He was the most interesting, determined and noble man I have ever known.

Our father worked hard and gave everything he had to the end. He survived many illnesses with patience and courage. He lived a dignified life and left us with dignity. We were with him, holding his hand – eyes forever closed on this world – as he peacefully took his last breaths, for his spirit to be reborn.

Like anyone who has lost someone they love and feel safe with, we will miss him every day and we will miss everything we learned from him. A man of few words, when he did speak, it was usually to share some truth or wisdom.

He once told us, "Health is lost, half is lost. Wealth is lost, nothing is lost. Character is lost, all is lost."

As a family, we will cherish the joyous moments we were fortunate to have, where we felt tranquillity in his presence and just knowing he was there. We hope to honour his example of duty and service in the work we do for the community and causes that need it.

Thank you for your thoughts and prayers for our father and family.

"Telle est la vie des hommes. Quelques joies, très vite effacées par d'inoubliables chagrins. Il n'est pas nécessaire de le dire aux enfants." – Marcel Pagnol

"We were promised sufferings. They were part of the programme. We were even told, 'Blessed are they that mourn,' and I accept it. I've got nothing that I hadn't bargained for. Of course it is different when the thing happens to oneself, not to others, and in reality, not imagination…The death of a beloved is an amputation." – C.S. Lewis.

— *20 October 2016* —

In loving memory of Tom Bedecarré

17 JANUARY 1956 — 29 MARCH 2025

AKQA co-founder, visionary and irreplaceable friend

It's appropriate, really, that although this book carries my name, it was somebody else's idea. It's fitting too that, though it is only now, in the final stages of editing, that I'm confident of its worth, somebody else saw its value before it was even begun.

That somebody was not just anybody. It was Tom Bedecarré. In 2023, as the 30th anniversary of the company we had nurtured approached, Tom sent me a string of messages. I should, he said, plan a new book: a book to celebrate what AKQA had become, the thousands of people who had been part of its success, and the millions of lives our work had touched.

"There are so many highlights," he wrote – alluding to industry milestones, awards, landmark projects, brilliant people – that it all needed to be celebrated. We should, he wrote, make a record of that work somewhere less ephemeral than the transient digital technologies where so much of it had thrived.

Tom kindly wrote that I was an open-spirited person whose achievements were built on generosity, and that it would be good for me to put my gratitude on paper. I listened to Tom's advice, as I always had. We were trusted partners to each other as we took the company global. Whether times were tough or triumphant, he was an unerring source of wisdom, calm, and reassurance.

Back in 2023, when Tom sent me those messages about what would become this book, neither of us could have guessed how things would look for us and AKQA a couple of years down the line. I had to say goodbye to the business I loved. I, and all of us who'd known and loved him, had to do the much harder job of saying goodbye to Tom.

As the great wave of responses I received as soon as I shared the following account of his passing proved, mine was but one of countless lives that Tom Bedecarré changed for the better.

"With deep sadness, I announce the passing of Tom Bedecarré, my beloved friend and fellow AKQA co-founder. Held in the grace and love of his three children, Tom left us peacefully on Saturday evening.

Tom brought joy, optimism, and a hopeful sense of possibility to every moment – and brightness to every life. His vision shaped a generation, but it was his heart and humanity that shaped us.

He was a rare and beautiful soul who made the world feel a little less cruel. With a single smile, Tom could remind you that life is still beautiful.

Tom was rightly called 'Silicon Valley's favourite ad man', but we knew him as our guide and mentor. He was a gracious and extraordinary man of courage – a person whose wisdom would steady, whose wit would heal, and whose compassion and kindness lifted us when we needed it most.

Tom's spirit runs through everything we are: the work we do, the lives we lead, and the quiet moments when we choose stillness over striving, kindness over pride, and empathy over ambition.

Tom, thank you for the love and the light. We'll carry it with us, always."

The Steve Jobs MBA

RELENTLESSLY IMPROVE EVERYTHING

How many companies do you know that would take a perfectly good operating system and then make lots of changes – most of them not noticeable, but which make computing faster, safer and more powerful? Apple did all of this with Snow Leopard.

ESCAPE THE EXECUTIVE IVORY TOWER

It's good for the CEO to reply to customer emails, as Jobs does. It shows – internally and externally – that the person at the top of the company cares about the consumer experience. Jobs doesn't let focus groups or committees rule over Apple, but he knows customer feedback is vital to improvements.

DON'T BOTHER TO CREATE MANIFESTOS, MANTRAS OR GUIDELINES – LIVE THEM

Big-statement documents are almost always pointless and dull. Put your thinking directly into action, so that all of your behaviour within your organisation becomes intuitive.

BENEFIT FROM LATE-MOVER ADVANTAGE

Not the first to bring an MP3 player, phone or tablet to market? Worry not – so long as you design a version that's an order of magnitude better than anything on the shelves. A late product that's excellent will always beat an early one that's mediocre.

BE ZEN, BE ORGANIC

Don't fight the natural order – embrace it. Nature often has the answers. The sunflower is the design inspiration for the iMac. If a product isn't beautiful, make it so. Put soul and humanity into what you make and its marketing and distribution.

OBSESS OVER DETAILS

Solve the problems other companies don't even know exist, or undertake challenges others consider impossible. Apple tackled the dilemma of people tripping over power cords by creating the MagSafe connector that disconnects when tugged. Find solutions that change the way consumers feel about and use your product.

ADD VALUE OR GET OFF THE TEAM

When Jobs returned to Apple in 1997, the company was on life support – its stock was at a 12-year low in Q2 of that year. The first step in his rescue plan was to remove all of the unnecessary overheads. If you ever bump into Steve Jobs in the corridor, you'd better have a good answer to the question, "What is it you do around here?"

LESS IS MORE

From corporate structure to design, minimalism wins every time. Take Apple's approach to packaging: less plastic and cardboard means reduced impact on the environment, lower shipping costs and not as much for the customer to carry. This all adds up to more margin – and happier consumers.

BE HANDS-ON

Get involved in the details, even if it drives your team crazy. And put your name on a few patents – Jobs has many, including one for the glass staircases within Apple stores. Attention to every detail of Apple's business means that Jobs is connected to every aspect of what the company does.

BE GENEROUS TO YOUR CUSTOMERS...

In how many places can you pay on the shop floor rather than going to a till? Apple stores might open at 9:00 a.m., but given that the queue for iPads can start at 5:30 a.m., Apple staff members arrive early and give customers a voucher enabling them to buy later in the day. Who else cares this much?

... BUT BE RUTHLESS WHEN IT COMES TO THE COMPETITION

If your competitors are shamelessly copying your ideas, take them out. Jobs has never been scared to mix it up, either internally or externally.

REMOVE CLUTTER

Whether in the engineering, the product, design, packaging, stores or the organisation, clutter is bad. Remove all that's extraneous until all that remains is absolutely necessary – and beautiful.

THE WORLD IS NOT ENOUGH

If you're not going to make your mark with a new product or idea, it's probably not worth launching. Apple is always and relentlessly about simply being the best at everything it does.

ACCESSIBILITY IS EVERYTHING

Making every product and aspect of the brand accessible doesn't mean that it isn't premium. Apple has mastered this by making its products so easy and intuitive to use that they don't need instruction manuals.

STAY HUNGRY, STAY FOOLISH

Steve Jobs quoted an issue of the *Whole Earth Catalog* in an address he gave to graduating Stanford students in June 2005. The quote says it all: "Stay hungry. Stay foolish."

First published in Wired *magazine in July 2011*

Remembering Dan Wieden

Dear Team,

With deep sadness, I learned this evening that Dan Wieden, co-founder of Wieden+Kennedy, passed away on Friday. Dan was 77 and died peacefully with his wife by his side.

With his razor-sharp wit and piercing wisdom, Dan was an extraordinary inspiration to me. His company became the world's most influential advertising agency. As the largest independent, it paved the way, proving that size and skilfulness can be symbiotic.

At a time when many question consumerism, the attitude Dan set in motion is work that's often more memorable than the products it promotes. But in our field, it is silence, not economics, that is the real wrong.

Nike's founder famously introduced himself to Dan's agency with the declaration, "I'm Phil Knight, and I hate advertising." Dan would defy convention to present a major reassessment of what the profession could be. He enabled Nike to discover its voice and use the power of that voice to build bridges, break boundaries, right injustices, correct societal wrongs and redress prejudices – all the while inspiring more people to exercise.

We shared clients, geographies and awards. We also shared an ethos. At one point, we even had conversations about merging AKQA into W+K. During one of these discussions, Dan gave me a tour of his stunning HQ in Portland, Oregon. I complimented him on the building. He spoke softly for someone who created a culture of exceptional work that makes so much noise. "The question is, who really owns this place?" he asked me. "You do, Dan," I earnestly replied. Realising from his less than effusive expression that – as an apprentice – I had given the wrong answer, I corrected myself with a more considerate response: "The people do, Dan. It's for everyone." At this, the brightness reappeared in his eyes.

Dan always understood the inner bond that draws one person to another. He has given generations of artists, writers and directors a canvas. Despite his agency's phenomenal success and immeasurable contribution, Dan never lost track of the dignity of the human soul. He said, "We need to get to kids who have no idea what we do. We need to open the doors wide and let them in. There are many undiscovered voices out there – voices that, against all odds, can rise up and enrich this culture and perhaps change the very nature of the marketplace for the better."

From our hearts, in honour and remembrance of Dan Wieden – who helped shape the course of the modern industry and so many careers, including mine.

Ajaz.

— Email sent 3 October 2022 —

Acceptance speech, honorary degree: doctor of business administration

In December 2018, Ajaz Ahmed was awarded an honorary degree at the University of Bath. Below is Professor Nancy Pucinelli's oration to the university's chancellor, followed by the recipient's speech

ORATION, PROFESSOR NANCY PUCINELLI

'Chancellor, I would like to tell you a story. Two undergraduates meet on the bus from the university into town as they head for a night out. Little did they know that only a handful of years later one of them would be starting a business and would persuade the other to join him. The two undergraduates were Ajaz Ahmed and Simon Jefferson. The business, AKQA, would go on to become the 2000-employee strong digital marketing leader from Amsterdam to Auckland. In 2012, it was valued at £350 million by Sir Martin Sorrell. Simon Jefferson graduated from the BBA programme to become the managing director of AKQA San Francisco.

I have had the great pleasure of speaking with Simon about the early days of working with Ajaz. Simon said that above all there were three words that capture the impact Ajaz has had not only on marketing but also on the many people who have been fortunate enough to work with him. Simon also thought these words would make Ajaz smile: "Courage to Care".

In 1997, Ajaz sent out an email to his entire company entitled, "The Courage to Care". Still in his early 20s, the message showed a foresight beyond his years. The following is a brief excerpt from that email.

"…the courage to care is about taking responsibility for projects, because you have enough pride in that project to ensure it is the best it can possibly be … not because we have to, but because we want to. Because it is the right thing to do."

While Ajaz urged his colleagues to care about clients and the projects of those clients, he always embraced this same courage. As I have learned about all that Ajaz has done for so many, it has become clear to me that the courage to care has permeated every aspect of his approach to leadership. His courage to care for his employees was shown in the early days by genuine recognition of their hard work. For instance, he rewarded the start-up team of 60 with a trip to New York for the weekend. More recently, he has maintained AKQA team culture by letting the media believe that the business's name, AKQA, comes from All Known Questions Answered and not Ajaz's initials.

Beyond his employees, Ajaz founded the AKQA Future Academy, a cohort-based development residency. While a traditional internship programme would most likely have been easier to organise and contribute more to AKQA's bottom line, Ajaz crafted an opportunity for significant professional development instead. And as if working on projects such as this alongside running his company was not enough, he took the time to personally engage with Academy participants. Ajaz's support of BBA alumnus Ben Wylie propelled Ben to build Cue Glasses that create artificial intelligence for the visually impaired and to build an Africa technology accelerator, The Baobab Network.

Ajaz has shown relentless commitment to the University of Bath, recruiting students and graduates and paying personal attention to their growth. He comes to campus to help groups such as Bath Entrepreneurs and funds prizes for the MSc e-Marketing module.

Chancellor, I present to you Ajaz Ahmed MBE, who is eminently worthy to receive the degree of doctor of business administration, *honoris causa*.'

ACCEPTANCE SPEECH, AJAZ AHMED

Your Royal Highness, Graduates, Ladies and Gentlemen,

My memories of Bath are wonderful memories. Bath is a beautiful, vibrant and happy city. My time here is always enchanting, enriching and full of joy. I'm fortunately reminded of that each time I'm lucky to have reason to visit.

The University of Bath is recognised and respected worldwide for its academic rigour, research, sports and cultural leadership.

Graduates of the University have the opportunity and are inspired, to make contributions of major significance to organisations and communities all over the world.

It was at the University of Bath that the kindness, intelligence and enthusiasm from the students and faculty introduced me to new technology. Moreover, it was this introduction that encouraged me to pursue a new journey as an entrepreneur.

The University of Bath has been a training ground for me and the many conscientious, capable and committed individuals who also went on to pursue their careers with us. I know we are an organisation that can better serve needs because of the high calibre of Bath University graduates.

I feel tremendously privileged to have attended the university and to have made lifelong friends, three of whom are with me here today: Richard John, Simon Willard and Simon Jefferson. Without their encouragement and serendipitous interventions, there wouldn't be an AKQA.

Likewise, we all stand on the shoulders of giants.

It is profound that for the first time in history we have enough cumulative knowledge, wealth and technology to create a sense of harmony and solve the world's conflicts and challenges. We also know that the most powerful force in the universe isn't technology, it's imagination.

Education and wisdom are the great equalisers.

These are the springboards to creating a better future. Education and wisdom are not just a preparation for life, but they are life itself, providing limitless opportunities, especially when you commit yourself to be a lifelong learner.

Over the course of my career, I've been fortunate to have had many job titles, but the best position I've ever been granted is Dad. It's a lifelong dedication to love, respect, duty and service.

Being a parent is the biggest honour and most positively transformative aspect of my life. We think we look after our kids, but in reality, they look after us.

It reminds me of the ancient proverb, "We do not inherit the Earth from our ancestors – we borrow it from our children."

Like anything we borrow, it's our responsibility to hand it back better than we found it.

Thank you for this honour. It is my pleasure to be associated with this remarkable institution.

This honorary doctorate is a gift that serves as a testament to the values and compassion of my parents; the kindness and generosity of my friends; and the commitment and ingenuity of my team.

PESSIMISM IS A PRISON THAT PERPETUATES ITSELF BY PARALYSING OUR WILL TO ACT

A cultural algorithm is never going to exist because if everyone used the same formula, all the output would also be

There are thousands of books written about leadership but it's really only about one thing:

Being a
decent
human
being.

Instead
of asking

"*Who* do we
compete *with*?"

should we
be asking

"*What* do we
compete *for*?"

My story demonstrates that it's possible to go from destitution, to aspiration, to contribution in one generation when a young person is given the chance to dream beyond their circumstances, the courage to rise above them, and the opportunity to make their mark upon the world.

The
best
work
is
always
an
invitation.

Everyone here is a trustee – a trustee for humanity and for our planet.

OWN THE DAY. OR LET THE DAY OWN YOU. YOU CAN BE THE ARCHITECT OF YOUR LIFE, OR MERELY THE TENANT.

5

Brands
& Values

Digital closed the gap between 'branding' and being.
Businesses who walked it like they talked it made it work

The brand is dead, long live the brand

Brands are vital to businesses online. But the online world makes traditional brand building all but impossible. It's time to do some reinventing.

Call it the brand paradox. On the one hand, new media makes a strong brand essential to any business. Companies without one will simply be lost in the torrents of information now surging across the world's networks. On the other hand, new media also pulls apart the traditional building blocks of the brand. Today's brands offer the customer a way of becoming informed about products, embracing a lifestyle, joining a community and entering into a relationship, all wrapped up together. New media changes the way in which customers approach all of these things so dramatically that building – or even maintaining – traditional brands becomes next to impossible.

Just a quick brush with the web demonstrates that brand advertising does not translate from old media into new. Even if the web had sufficient bandwidth to carry video to every PC in the world, television advertisements could still only be put onto websites as ironic comment. The shouting, jingle-chanting and brand-name blasting needed to imprint information on the brain of a couch potato wondering where his next snack will come from just sound ridiculous when presented to a mouse-clicking net surfer. Even relatively weighty corporate brochures look trivial, boring and unconvincing on screen, particularly when compared to the masses of fast-changing information on the web.

It's not surprising that advertising should fail to translate. Brands were created for producers, to enable factory builders and assembly-line innovators to tout the virtues of their newly mass-produced wares to the mass markets they hoped and prayed were waiting to receive them. The web, by contrast, was created for consumers, to provide a way of picking through – and making individual sense of – masses of information and goods. The new medium not only implies a change of viewpoint but also, by definition, enables a complete change in the way in which brand advertising carries out its various functions.

Existing media force brand-builders to mix together information and persuasion, fact and emotion, community-building and customer service all into a single, compact piece of work. New media provides more room to manoeuvre, and more tools to manoeuvre with. Indeed, the first act in the process of reinventing the brand is to deconstruct it. Only by breaking brands into constituent parts can marketers give each part the depth required to make a success in this world of new media.

In effect, the web unbundles advertising. webvertising must provide real answers to real questions, not canned information; it must offer interactions that satisfy real needs, not blanket persuasions; it must create communities that actually speak to one another, not just content itself with aspirations. And these processes do not necessarily, or ideally, all take place together. Sites that provide information about a product's features and benefits have to be separated from those that attempt to satisfy consumers' aspirations by building a community around the brand for the like-minded to join. Both further distinguish themselves from sites that try to create a direct relationship between buyers and sellers and from sites that take a multimedia approach to enhancing a brand's image.

THE COMPLETE BRAND ENVIRONMENT

Eventually, the various constituents of brand building should logically recombine. Instead of an advertising campaign, the web offers ways to build a complete brand environment – one which combines product information, a stylish image, community-building and a direct relationship to the producer, all packaged in a way that resonates with the values and style of the brand itself. But that is still a long way off for most brands, and not all products will need all of these constituent elements.

In the meantime, would-be web brand-builders need to ask themselves what would do most to help sell their product now. More information about the product's technical features and the benefits of using it? A direct relationship between company and customer? Intimations that the product will help the consumer to join a community of attractive people? Or just some bright, breezy imagery to remind would-be buyers of the brand's emotional values? The following examples show how pushing the possibilities along only one of these dimensions can transform a brand.

BEER, CHOCOLATE AND JEANS

Carling lager is not, at first glance, the brand most likely to prosper on the web. Putting screens full of information about the brewing process onto the web is unlikely to shift more pints of lager. So the brand's site tries to build a community by focusing on one of the beer drinker's other favourite pastimes: football.

Carling's ability to talk football is bolstered by the fact that it sponsors the Premier League, so it can get teams to participate in its site. Indeed, the teams provide much of the information on the site, which is full of facts about players, results of games and news of the league; there's little mention of lager. Fans can swap football opinions in electronic discussion groups. They can also order football merchandise.

Confectionery company Mars also decided to build a community around shared interests with the Snickers site. As chocolate eaters are less easy to stereotype than lager drinkers, the company encourages them to define themselves. According to the developer, Hyperinteractive, 90 per cent of the content for the site is generated by users submitting reviews and opinions. Publication is speedy; once a visitor has sent an email about a movie or soccer game, for example, it's moderated and online within 30 minutes. Surprisingly, people seem quite willing to gather around a chocolate bar for a natter.

Diesel and Levi's show the possibilities of the web for building brand image. Both brands have focused much of their conventional advertising on creating a personality for their products. Levi's uses the web as an extension of television advertising. Diesel adds more irony to its site to appeal to a younger, hipper, more British audience. It promises "beautiful, dysfunctional cheerleaders", and illustrates the site with the same striking graphics and postmodern lounge lizards that populate its advertisements.

THE TOTAL BRAND EXPERIENCE

Of all the constituents of brand building, though, image creation takes least advantage of the interactivity of the web. Few sites have translated image into experience, so image-building on the web is still largely a passive experience. If nothing else, measuring the payoffs of image-building is extremely difficult, adding to the problems of justifying websites that try to do just that.

Information-oriented sites, by contrast, automatically provide market research to those companies smart enough to gather it. By tracking the information that surfers request, companies can improve their knowledge of would-be customers' concerns. The most obvious candidates for information-oriented web support are companies with complicated products. Computers and software, both of which are complicated, are obvious candidates for websites – and most high-tech firms already tell you everything you might want to know about their products via the web.

But it's also possible to add information to a product that might not at first glance seem to call for it. When we at AKQA built a site for Durex condoms, we stressed information about sex. Today, smart sex is safer sex, and vice versa. So the Durex site is set up to answer questions about sexual health and contraception, often anonymously.

The classic customer-service site is Federal Express. Some 15,000 FedEx customers visit the site each day to locate parcels in transit with FedEx; type in your tracking number and the site queries FedEx's computers to find out where it is. FedEx wins three ways from the site.

It saves around US$2 million (£1.3 million) a year by getting customers to query the computer directly instead of telephoning a FedEx employee. By making its internal processes more visible, it boosts its reputation for quality. And it has improved the service itself: companies can reassure dubious customers that the cheque really is in the post by pointing them to the website.

BMW's website, another AKQA development, also focuses on customer service. It allows a customer to locate their local BMW dealer by typing in their postcode, and it can search BMW's nationwide list of used cars. Customers can also book a test drive or send off for brochures. BMW tracks the sales leads that the site generates; in the first few months of operation, sales of cars to customers who came to BMW via the website more than repaid the investment required to create it.

At BMW, though, customer service doesn't stand alone. The site also has to maintain the car's luxury image and to provide product details for a wide range of models. To do this, it has tried to bring together on the site some of the other brand-building functions, to begin to create a total brand experience. As a start towards community-building, for example, the site features competitions. Eventually, BMW hopes to expand the site into a complete environment for the BMW brand.

USING THE WEB – NOT VICE VERSA

There's no single formula for a successful website. What successful sites do have in common, though, is that they focus on the brand, not on the web. Executives often find the web's vast possibilities seductive and are tempted to stray from their own business into some form of publishing. Given that most publishers are themselves struggling to make sense of the economics of web publishing, this can only lead to disappointment. Successful webvertisers, by contrast, have asked not what they can do on the web but what the web can do for them – be it providing information, creating a relationship with the customer, building community or just boosting the brand's image.

And they have measured it. The interactivity of the web offers more than just new ways of communicating a brand's own message. For those smart enough to listen – and it can be surprisingly hard to convince marketing executives to do so, given the assumption they've inherited from old media that brand building is an output-only exercise – interactivity provides a way of measuring customers' own expectations of the brand and the way they react to it. At the very least, this interaction can show whether or not a website is paying its way. More ambitiously, interactivity will make advertising an integral part of the products themselves; brand advertising and the experience of using the product will merge.

This change will require companies to define more clearly the values that underlie the brand and to instil them throughout the firm – since everyone who interacts with a customer will effectively become part of the brand. But in approaching the web, executives have to start asking the question that will remain at the top of their agendas throughout this transformation: what new capabilities and services will enhance the value of our branded product to our customers? That is the ultimate lesson of the web. It's not what sounds good or looks cool that ultimately matters – it's what works.

— *First published in* Wired *magazine in April 1995* —

A public announcement: advertising is over

Planning a start-up and wondering how much of your limited budget to allocate to traditional advertising? We have no doubt of the answer: nothing. Though they shouldn't, traditional advertising and mass media still dominate many marketing budgets.

That made sense when the networks open to companies – billboards, cinemas, newspapers and TV – were owned by a handful of broadcasters and publishers. Brands paid outside 'creatives' lots of money to come up with dazzling campaigns, then paid outside media buyers to pay media owners even more money in order to get them seen. It was the only way.

Not any more. The traditional gatekeepers are still here, but they are no longer the only people with keys. As *Wired* readers are well aware, new ideas and businesses now reach us through the mobile web, apps, social media and numerous other digital channels. A well-defined project from the funding platform Kickstarter is just as much about seeding an innovative new idea or company in the public imagination as it is about raising money. And that is just the first of three crucial structural shifts that digital has facilitated and which disrupt the very idea of advertising.

For the consumer, digital has changed things even more drastically. The phone is the passport to everything advertising was designed to obscure – which is to say, the truth. Fifteen years ago, the only way to differentiate between brands of washing-up liquid was to fall for the claims made for them in their ads. Today, you can get the real views of millions of people, and the opinions of your friends, by consulting the device in your pocket. Sure, the brand might still have an outdoor campaign, a catchy jingle or a groovy strapline – but compared to the meaningful data that we can instantly access today, that's just hissing in the wind. Thanks to that, ad campaigns that tell fibs, create myths or overhype products get exposed and ridiculed instantly; a campaign can be reduced to a joke in an afternoon on Twitter.

Now, it's wisest to ensure that whatever you might call 'promotion' actually substantiates the value of your product, not mythologises it. The third reason digital has made old-fashioned 'advertising' redundant? The very idea of outsourcing 'creative' thinking to *Mad Men*-style mavericks is out of date. Brands should know their businesses and customers better than anybody. In a digital world, their job is to build from that knowledge by collaborating with, not commissioning, talent from beyond.

Collaboration is a much more powerful way of understanding how to serve your customer and their desires. Talk value is worth more than any ad. 'Serve the customer'? We know some readers will be sniggering at the back there. But if you think about it, brands no longer have a choice.

It's no accident that the most successful companies today have established themselves through indispensable services, not shallow promises. Their low-key, how-it-works, soft-sell approaches that refuse to insult the intelligence of their audiences are about delivering true value. 'Here's something we think is cool, maybe you'll like it.' Nobody knows your business and your customer better than you. Use the power of digital to find new ways to create love and loyalty. Make marketing a part of the development process, not an afterthought. Most importantly, make something brilliant. As Jeff Bezos says, "Advertising is the price you pay for having an unremarkable product or service." The premise is that today we have a new communication platform, when in reality what we have is a new connection platform based around what matters in people's lives.

It's an opportunity to make yourself indispensable. And that's not an ad brief.

— First published in Wired *magazine in June 2012 —*

Time flies, trends change. True classics get better with age

80s brands are today's hottest tickets. Not for being old but because they're pure gold

From TikTok taking over to lunch-break Botox booking, the evidence is everywhere. Today's culture is, as ever, captivated by the enchanting allure of youth. Yet in the spring of 2023, middle-aged brands seem to be everywhere. This season's sensation on Apple TV+ is *Tetris*, a dramatisation of the early history of a 39-year-old video game. At the cinema, *Super Mario Bros.*, a celebration of a computer game character first seen in 1981, is breaking box-office records. *Air*, an origin story of sports drama and legendary footwear design set in 1984, courts large audiences.

Analysts and commentators speculate if this wave of nostalgia is a relatable balm for a pandemic-weary world eager to reaffirm community bonds, a cosy retreat into childhood comfort zones, or simply the latest instalment of a standard cycle of sentimentality where kids from 30 to 40 years ago have grown up into senior positions of influence today.

There's probably some truth to all these theories. But perhaps we risk overlooking a more obvious point: venerable brands are not having a moment because they're old. They're glowing because they're golden. Don't call it a comeback because – never having been bettered – none actually went away. Far from being rooted or trapped in their beginnings, these remarkable creations remain relevant through iteration and innovation.

Tetris has been ported to more platforms than any other game. *Tetris Effect* is one of the most exciting things you can do with a cutting-edge VR rig, and psychologists have shown that 'The Tetris Effect', whereby your mind becomes entirely focused on managing the ever-accelerating flow of falling blocks, is uniquely effective in treating post-traumatic stress.

The 'Mario Universe' has spawned more than 30 megahits. With over 50 million copies purchased, *Mario Kart 8 Deluxe* is the bestselling title on Nintendo's console. Why? Because not one rival down the years has come close to being as much fun.

Air Jordan not only brought Michael and basketball to the global stage but also served as the catalyst for the modern sneaker cult. Reissues of classics have been instant sellouts, and just this week, a pair of Jordan 13s once worn by His Airness sold for a record $2.2 million at auction.

Time-honoured brands renew and adapt with their audiences. The best do that without forgetting the essence of what made them special. In his book *Hit Makers*, Derek Thompson shows how success in any creative field hinges on balancing the human desire for what's new and intriguing with our yearning for the recognisable and familiar.

When your brand is still best in class, you can't be accused of living in the past.

— First published in April 2023 —

The end is nigh for identikit advertising

It has never been easier for people to scan past, tune out or switch over, so to persist with identikit advertising campaigns is ridiculous.

One of the biggest challenges facing all organisations today is the ability to consistently coordinate and amplify a single brand voice across all media. At the same time, given the myriad of options available, it's somewhat ridiculous to expect audiences to automatically pay attention to identikit, predictable advertising because it's never been easier for consumers to scan past work created for the lowest common denominator.

While there will always be new ideas, platforms, services and devices, one lasting truth is that people only have a short attention span when they're bored.

We have audiences raised on social networks – ones which have become operating systems for their lives: living databases for their memories and an instant way to share their thoughts across geographies and time zones. People have access to so much dynamic media and technology that they have become experts at filtering and managing it, the result being that audiences are far more discretionary because they can dramatically edit what media they choose to spend time with.

At the same time, the media itself is becoming more intelligent at curating content. Set-top boxes and complex remote controls are merely irritating interim steps towards a more intelligent, clutter-free TV experience. Voice and gesture will become an interface for the big screen in your home.

Smart TV doesn't just mean connected to the internet so you can have access to any content, social networks or make video calls. It also means users can access a vault of digital content, family photos, videos and music. The real intelligence will be in a digital concierge that will help organise lives, moving with users seamlessly depending on the device they're using at the time.

The year 2012 should be one defined by ideas that leap out and command attention – remarkable works that people want to share. Great brands have always been about smart and artful storytelling. Great agencies have always given brands a vision of what they could be – and technology pushes things forward.

It's created a level playing field where good partners have permission to orchestrate a brand's messages in all media because audiences ultimately decide how they feel about a brand by evaluating all of its messages: the product or service and the conversations about it, its internet or mobile message, in shops or through new devices.

In the art of persuasion, nothing is more powerful than an understanding of what instincts dominate a person's actions and what compulsions drive them. For advertising agencies and media owners to stay relevant, they must broaden their scope, especially in those they employ. Agencies and media owners also need to expand their frames of reference to include what's influential today and what will be important tomorrow so that their work is culture-creating and genre-defining.

Organisations must embrace the responsibility of ensuring business is ethical, likeable and interesting to young people as the new generation's focus is less on status and more on sustainability. The challenge is to ensure their philosophical approach is about the audience wanting to applaud the work for having the best ideas.

For a development team, it's about a process of rigorous examination to perfect the product and the experience.

For our part, as an independent agency that is now well into its second decade of existence, we cannot and have never been reliant on hand-me-down relationships from a larger holding group. We've had to take responsibility and earn the opportunity to work on every assignment. In other words, we must value our values.

— First published in The Guardian *in February 2012 —*

Interface is the brand, so let the glory days of story begin

Whether we are gathered around a campfire, a cathode ray tube or an iPad, it's the story that's being shared that matters

In our digitally driven world, the pace and power with which life and work change can feel overwhelming at times. With all that information, evolution and revolution out there, it's all too easy for any one of us to feel off the pace and nervous about the future.

If I sense my mind heading that way, I know exactly how to regroup my thoughts and fix things. I look away from the latest software updates and NASDAQ sensations and towards a timeless source of clarity and consolation: the story.

Whether we've gathered round a campfire, a cathode ray tube, a plasma screen or an iPad to share them, humans have always encoded the important stuff into the form of stories. From the beginnings of human speech, narrative gave us a form in which to pass on advice, information and inspiration.

As human culture evolved, folk tales were the means by which our ancestors hoped to help their descendants to catch the woolly mammoth, escape the dark forest and live happily ever after. Then, as literacy spread, plays, poems and novels passed on these learnings.

As was then, the stories that now spread are the ones with the greatest emotional resonance. Today, at my company AKQA, we talk about "telling stories through software" as the latest incarnation of that essential human habit.

Simply put, the interface is the brand. A compelling story is the best way to cut through the sheer mass of choice, data and distraction in our lives today.

In a digital world, it's all too easy for a business to forget the person at the other end of its service. Equally, it's incredibly easy for that person to click to something more meaningful if your stories are forgettable and unremarkable.

For these reasons, you could argue that stories matter more to us today than ever. Others certainly do – think about how often you've heard CEOs, politicians and celebrities talk about the importance of 'getting our story right' or launching a 'new narrative' to improve their lives or even change the world.

It's easy to talk about story, but it's hard to do it well. That has always been the case, but there are extra challenges when you do it digitally. The starting point should be the truth, and that's because today's world is so transparent – everybody has access to peer opinion and objective advice through the smartphone in their pocket. If you want to tell fairy tales, people are going to call you out publicly on the gap between what you say and what you do.

Just as the first stories helped early humans solve day-to-day problems, apps today take people on a narrative journey and, at the same time, solve life's little problems for them.

When it introduced Timeline, Facebook moved from a 'noticeboard' archetype to a narrative one, giving page owners the power to tell their own life stories through the terms and things they deemed most important.

We can also learn from video games. Thanks to iPhones, everyone and their grandmother is now a gamer, so it's a perfect time for companies to use technology in an intelligent, people-focused way to make the customer more than just a passive audience for your story.

If the *Mad Men* era is dead, then long live the new era of 'The Long Tale', where the enduring quality of your story matters more than the relentlessness of your promotional spend. That's not an unhappy ending.

— First published in The Guardian in June 2012 —

It's never too late to pivot and revive a brand

AKQA's founder says brands that champion what really matters to people will always have a future – but ditching any emotional attachment is the first step to achieving revival

Ever since the start of the current global downturn, a new type of list has started making its way into those ubiquitous New Year predictions features. This kind of list is typically introduced along such lines as: "companies most likely to go bust". It usually involves an expert analyst unveiling their tally of the struggling household name businesses that the statistical indicators say will fail soonest. (It's a somewhat staggering fact that 87 per cent of companies in the Fortune 500 in 1955 were no longer in existence by 2011.)

This extinction prediction game is an understandable impulse in changing times – in recent years, we've become as used to nostalgically waving off what we thought were bulletproof brands as we have to welcoming exciting new digital brands.

But there are more valuable ways to respond when you see a company whose existence in danger. Especially if you look at it from the point of view of the soon-to-be-out-of-work employee, rather than the clever commentator reading the runes. Entrepreneurial thinking is surely characterised by maximising available resources. Surely, it would be smarter not to consign a company to its doom, but rather to help it find a way to redirect its energy; refocus; and settle on a new, future-proofed direction.

I certainly think so, because I believe it's never too late for any company, of whatever size, to turn on its axis and confidently charge in a new direction. The ability to envision a new, smarter way of doing things has always been a hallmark of great entrepreneurs, and the pivot – as we'll call such a manoeuvre – has been the defining act in the history of many famous firms.

In a world gone digital, the rewards for those who pivot at the right time are – like the penalties for those who refuse to – accelerated and amplified. In the most well-known contemporary cases, the change-around stemmed from good digital principles: acknowledging that competition has left your Plan A in the dust, being open to new ideas and responding to what interests your audience.

So Burbn – a Foursquare-like location service that took a year to develop but was still fiddly and behind the curve – was quickly remade into the highly accessible photo-sharing app Instagram. Twitter was sparked by a 2006 brainstorming exercise at podcast company Odeo, in response to the new threat of iTunes. Flickr started out as an image solution for an online game that was being built, before taking over from it. Woot was sold to Amazon for $110 million, but it started out as an ad hoc solution to sell off a store's old stock of electronics components online.

Admirable and crucial as all those decisions were, it's hard not to see the great analogue-era pivots as even bolder. Rather than spending investors' money at a start-up, the 20th century's great masters of the pivot were often risking decades of brand equity and family savings when they set out in a new direction.

Miuccia Prada had trained in theatre and earned a doctorate in political science before she took on the family luxury luggage business her grandfather set up. Seven years after taking on the company, she initiated the Prada pivot with a range of nylon bags. These rewrote the codes of luxury and paved the way for the Milan company to become a global fashion powerhouse. An outsider who had previously regarded fashion as 'dumb' had brought her intellect and family expertise together to inaugurate a new era for the industry.

When fashion conglomerate Limited Brands bought the ailing Abercrombie & Fitch name in 1988, it achieved a comparable feat. It managed to remake an ailing sporting and outdoors equipment store into a brand that merely evoked the outdoors life. Responding to a changing world, they went from serious products for a pastime to a new kind of clothing, which was more about suggesting an aspirational lifestyle than equipping people for the wild life.

After the Pixar Image Computer launched in 1986, John Lasseter would produce animated demos to show off its high-performance graphic capabilities. Within a few years, those demos became the blueprint for Pixar's future. They'd gone from engineering hardware for digital artists to becoming storytellers in software (and the most lauded studio of modern times) themselves.

Talking of toy stories, Hassenfeld Brothers was a textile remnant company for decades, then quietly moved into school and dressing-up equipment for kids. In 1952, they bought the rights to a design for a Mr Potato Head, became Hasbro and made history.

Berkshire Hathaway was another textiles company – before Warren Buffett, originally just an investor, stepped in and future-proofed it as a finance firm. Consider how Nokia went from the 19th-century merger of a rubber and paper company to making electricity cables and, later, networks and phones. They found global fame in a field far removed from their origins, yet the key elements of their DNA can be traced all the way back.

Nokia could probably do with another pivot now. They could look at how record label moguls and musicians Dr Dre and Jimmy Iovine made cabling work for them. They knew that, although the old ways they had made money from were dying along with record sales, people still loved great music, celebrities and pop stars. They also knew, from the iPod earbud example, that headphones were usually chosen as much for style as sound.

So they teamed up with hi-fi cable firm Monster Cable to launch a range of premium, pop star-endorsed headphones with a bold aesthetic signature. And, of course, they made many millions in an industry otherwise full of people feeling the pinch.

Rather than worrying about becoming redundant, they pivoted by championing what they knew actually mattered to people. Pivoting is about getting to the essence and foregoing the fluff – often, you can't get to where you need to go until you've shed every bit of excess baggage and sentimental attachment.

Once that's done, you can assess what you've really got and figure out how to work it. The eternal human attributes – storytelling and sex appeal – will always hold great value for people. They will always have great potential for pioneering and profitable ideas, whatever else changes. Drill down to the emotions that matter. When it comes to working out how great companies can stay great by changing direction, the only feeling to fear is fear itself.

— First published in The Guardian *in January 2013 —*

We exist
to put
multi-
mediocrity
out of its
misery

THE
INTERFACE
BRAND
IS THE

THE MOST
SUCCESSFUL
PEOPLE

ARE THE ONES WHO HELP OTHERS SUCCEED THE MOST

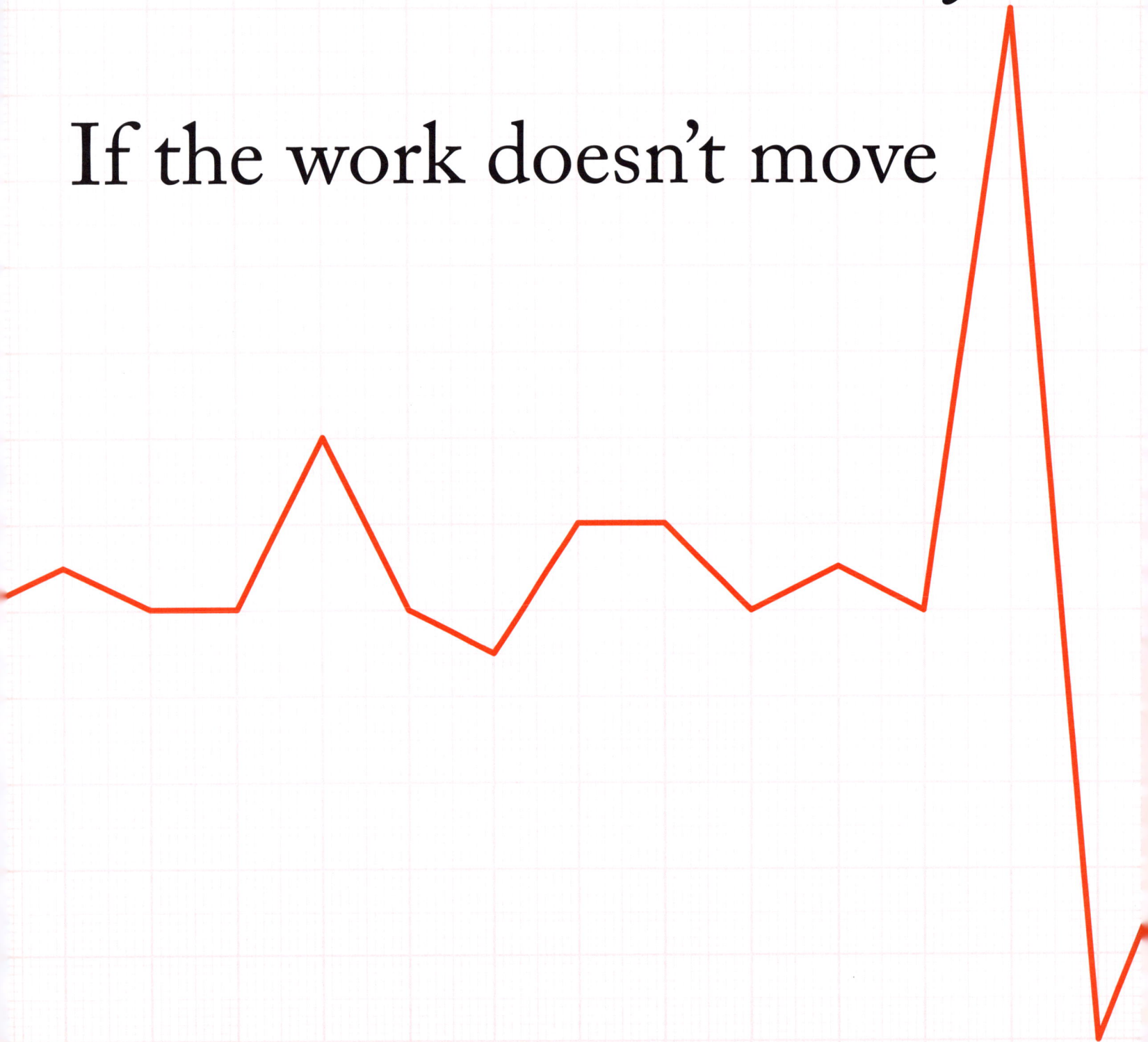

If the work doesn't move *you*

it won't move the market

We think we
look after our kids,
but in reality, they
look after us.

Art and entrepreneurship are two expressions of one shared desire: to leave the world a little different than you found it.

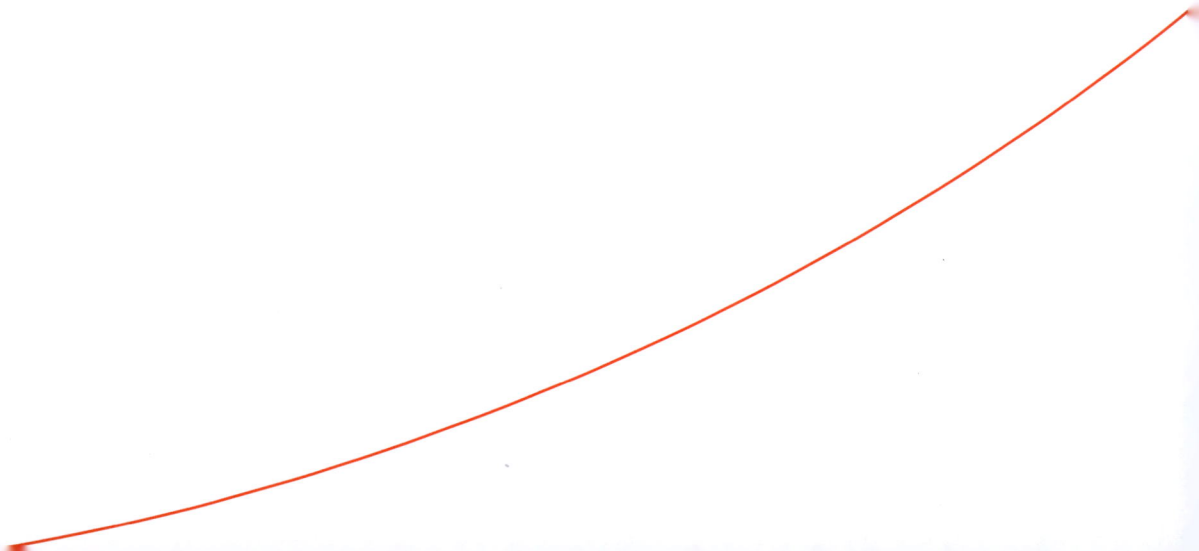

If we fear to be wrong, we fear taking risks, and if we can't subvert, then we can't pioneer.

You have to stay hungry as satisfaction is the first step towards decline.

6

Dreams & Discipline

To create the best work, you need to balance restraint, relentless rigour and fearless imagination

Innovate or simplify?

The feature-length documentary *Rams* (2018) is full of beautiful things – namely, the designs of its subject Dieter Rams. The radios, blenders, calculators and coffee makers Rams created for Braun are as pleasing to look at and as covetable as when they were released half a century ago, which is no surprise given how his curved corners and uncluttered aesthetic have informed design in our smartphone era. But the documentary is full of sadness: the product design guru casting his eye over his countless 21st-century disciples and suggesting that, however much homage they pay to his stylistic hallmarks, many of them have missed the underlying point of it all.

You don't need to be familiar with Rams's ideas or his *Ten Principles for Good Design* to understand why, for all the adulation, he doesn't feel at home in our era of screen resolution arms races, annual hardware refreshes, novelty interfaces and daily phone charging duties. You just need to look at the products he oversaw, or better still, use one. Rams's objective was to make machines that did their jobs efficiently, unobtrusively and durably. We routinely call them 'iconic' now, but Rams's aim was less for them to stand out and more for them to disappear: to fit into our lives, to serve us so well and so long that we bought less stuff and created less pollution and waste, not more.

So if we're surrounded by surface signs of Rams's influence, what happened to the principles of good design that underpinned that pioneering work? Well, amongst other things, 'innovation' happened: not as a process, but as a cultural ideal. As we witnessed dorm-room start-ups becoming billion-dollar global forces, the innovator became the new paradigm of business success and personal aspiration. Innovation became a matter of national identity: governments invoked it to project rosy economic futures in the face of global competition. Meanwhile, the old, analogue language of 'design' increasingly receded into specialist corners: fashion, interiors or the rarefied world of luxury goods and old-style artisanship.

As someone who's always been excited by new technological possibilities, and who has sometimes been labelled an 'innovator', I don't mean to be ungrateful, or to sound like a luddite. But it's looks to me like a glut of 'innovation' is actually an indicator of a lack of 'good design'.

The two ideas certainly weren't synonymous to sociologist E.M. Rogers. Our contemporary terminology for the spread of new ideas and trends – 'influencers', 'early adopters' and the rest – derives from the 'Theory of Innovation' he published back in 1962, when the post-war consumer boom was in full swing and Dieter Rams was busy at Braun. Rogers argued that successful innovations weren't necessarily improvements on what they replaced. All that mattered was that enough of the right people thought they were improvements. Today, when the meme age has vastly accelerated the spread of such trends, and we're all too aware of how new alerts and enticements constantly vie for our precious attention, we're all too aware of our susceptibility to newness for newness' sake. Thanks to what one consumer electronics executive called the 'digital sashimi' life cycle of modern electronics, the device that was your pride and joy can swiftly become an embarrassment.

There are other reasons to resist the urge to champion innovation. It's not a preoccupation in the important events in our lives. 'Innovative' isn't the first compliment you'd pay someone who'd just conducted a heartrending Beethoven symphony, or (molecular gastronomists excepted) cooked you a delicious meal. And even though it garners the headlines and therefore looms large in discussions of business and economics, innovation only comprises a small part of any economy. The rest is the everyday nuts-and-bolts miracle of keeping society and its systems ticking along.

At its least appealing, 'innovation' is not even charming, merely annoying, because it makes life more complicated. If I go to a football match and want to send messages and movies to my friends and feeds or consult related websites, I am diverted to an innovative hub for fans. It would cost more to provide the additional bandwidth to allow me to use my phone as I liked, but it would be nice. And easier. If I travel on the public transport system in London, I see numerous cameras and hear plenty of warnings about safety and security, but I can't pretend that makes me feel more at ease than the human staff who used to keep watch so much more visibly. If I find myself driving an innovative car with a touch interface instead of an old-fashioned switchgear, I have to engage two of my senses to use it, instead of the old-fashioned one. (Just as, if I want to have a music player in my pocket which I can control without having to look at a screen, I have to seek out an antiques dealer who can get hold of a first-generation iPod.) Considering the low cost of the once-luxury touchscreen, we might see such innovations as euphemisms for cutting costs, which is some sort of excuse. Elsewhere, though, additional expense doesn't necessarily make innovation any better either.

We can argue over whether to call them 'elevators' or 'lifts', but we can agree that they're as costly to install and operate as ever, and more to the point, that all their complicated modern security features and systems mean they can seem slower and more confusing than ever. Companies make a big noise when they replace automated systems or cheap international call centres with innovative helplines, but more often than not, the outcome is the same. The average human interface still works on the remains of old call-centre tree-systems, so the benefit of having a nuanced, expensive human interlocutor is often lost to the same old binary frustrations. If a finance person tells me about an 'innovation in financial products', I know that it will be so complex that I probably won't understand it and that that will be the whole point of it.

It still surprises me when old acquaintances come over all fretful and fidgety the minute they're out of range of the wireless internet or a power supply. It's a reminder of how, while bad design lumbers us with extra duties that tie us down or cause us anxiety, good design strives to free us up.

Regardless of all this, a preference for 'innovation' is still baked into the language of politics and business; it's part of how CEOs talk to shareholders, a seeming obligation in a world of rapid refreshes and pressure to keep growing your profits. But for me, simplicity has always been a more useful touchstone. However new and shiny your invention, it's no good if it doesn't do what it is supposed to or if ordinary people can't figure out how to use it.

Even in the digital age, sustained success as often rests on human-centric simplification as much as it does on dramatic innovation: consider how today's technology titans first drew people in by offering a less busy, more accessible sanctuary for exchange.

Simplicity can be a key to longevity, too. That's not only because something built with no unnecessary complications and minimal moving parts is most likely to be more robust. It's also because the better and more liberating a tool you provide people with, the more likely they will be to make new uses for that tool, rather than discard it, when changes you didn't plan for affect their lives and habits.

There's a special thrill to be had from making something new, a sensation loaded with potential and unencumbered by failure: you can cherish the pleasure in the faces of people as you give them a first glimpse of your new idea; you can daydream about grander plans or rewards to come. But the simple satisfaction of making something as well as you possibly can is something else. If, after your daydreams have been dragged through the rubble of the real world, you persevere and graft and eventually build something that makes it all worthwhile, the satisfaction is little short of miraculous.

That was the theory behind the old apprenticeship system, where years of chores, failures and dangers would eventually see you ascend to the status of 'journeyman' and lead to a point where you, too, could create work worthy of your guild and their trusting customers. To become a 'master craftsman', the apprentice would have to flawlessly execute an exemplary specimen of the guild's craft. Sometimes this would allow for new ideas, but usually, the task was simply about completing a very difficult technical task whose completion depended on all your experience and knowledge of your materials. Centuries before the term was applied to such innovative rock albums, novelists or even paintings, that was the original meaning of making a 'masterpiece'.

We don't need to turn back the clock or forego the new tools we have. We shouldn't pretend that a chunk of code can't be as beautiful and practical as any old-school craftwork. Innovation isn't bad; it just isn't everything. If we can't stop reinventing the wheel, we don't merely risk failing to get any closer to our destination. We're also in very real danger of forgetting the destination altogether.

— Originally published in Defeat *in 2019 —*

How to launch new

This is the text of a speech given at a Royal Television Society event called 'Too Much to Watch?' which was held at King's College, Cambridge, in September 2023, where industry figures were invited to talk about the future of the media landscape

The competition for attention in this homogenous, media-saturated, media-abundant world – where there's a global pandemic of attention deficit disorder – has never been more intense.

How does one idea manage to capture the conversation, imagination and attention of the masses, while others vanish into oblivion and obscurity?

Taste used to be dictated top-down. The studios, broadcasters, gatekeepers and reviewers could pretty much decide what would be a hit using the power of distribution, schedules, control and exposure.

We now live in a bottom-up world where popularity is dictated by the masses. What this means is that spending millions on advertising doesn't necessarily guarantee that a product will become popular.

Although the previous system is not entirely obsolete, its influence has certainly fragmented and waned in comparison to the democratised, decentralised and diversified, but also derivative, landscape of today's cultural environment. It's a shift that's given individuals more agency and widened their perspective.

Despite the astonishing enthusiasm and overwhelming levels of hype, where artificial intelligence can seemingly solve all of humanity's problems, and at the same time apparently threatens our very existence, there isn't a shortcut to be taken. There isn't a code to be cracked, a puzzle to be solved or a 'cultural algorithm' to be programmed.

That's because formulas only ever work when the underlying variables don't change. But the ingredients that make something exciting and surprising change all the time, depending on who the audience is and when the idea is happening. We are all constantly getting new signals about what is good and what is popular, what is the new normal and what is inappropriate.

A foolproof formula for extraordinary success is never going to exist because if everyone used the same formula, all the output would also be the same.

An alternative approach might be to understand the time-tested ingredients of human affinity that make us click, and then overlay these with some fundamental principles to dramatically increase the likelihood of success.

According to Derek Thompson, author of the unsentimental and brilliant book *Hitmakers*, the key factor of popular cultural products is 'Familiar Surprises'. Thompson's thesis is this: "familiarity over novelty, and distribution over content," where he says: "to sell something surprising, make it familiar. But to sell something familiar, make it surprising."

The legendary godfather of industrial design, Raymond Loewy, who streamlined America with his bold and beautiful designs, put it another way with his theory called MAYA, which stands for Most Advanced, Yet Acceptable.

Influential factors that could be force multipliers and play a leading role in shaping what becomes popular incorporate elements that are familiar and relatable while also introducing something that's novel and unique to capture attention and interest.

Emotionality and familiarity are incredibly potent when it comes to popularising content, yet alone, they are insufficient. This underscores the importance of social influence, network effects, talkability and shareability. Despite the myth, fame doesn't happen by chance. There's no such thing as a 'viral phenomenon'; everything needs a nudge to launch it into the public consciousness.

The distribution strategy and mechanisms are as crucial as the content itself. Word of mouth is still the most valuable medium of all. 'New' also needs to be 'good' because the benefit of digital networks is that while they have the power to accelerate hits, the ideas that don't resonate will just fade faster.

Certain psychological triggers and emotional appeals can make a cultural product more appealing. These might include curiosity, nostalgia and the promise of pleasure or satisfaction.

The timing and cultural context surrounding a product's launch are equally pivotal in shaping its popularity. The prevailing cultural backdrop and trends can greatly influence the success of an idea and how it is perceived and received.

But, most of all, it's about the vision to question the status quo, and challenge the confines of convention by daring to disrupt the mundane and monotonous.

It's about the leadership to be an agent of change at the vanguard, not the old guard.

It's about the empathy to show respect for audiences by enriching, surprising, inspiring and entertaining.

The best work is always an invitation.

When new companies tap timeless values, consumers respond

Timeless values applied via new technology can democratise markets and extend access to experiences, goods and services

The trailer for the movie *The Internship* works for three reasons. First, the proven bromantic comedy duo of Vince Vaughn and Owen Wilson is reunited, older and no wiser. Second, audiences have what is likely first-hand experience with the basic premise – veteran employees who suddenly find not only their jobs but also their industry, facing extinction. Third, and most interestingly, the trailer works because everybody can empathise with the heroes' answer to their predicament: bag a job at Google.

It's a reminder of how – for all the drastic economic, technological and behavioural change it's experienced in recent times – American aspirational culture still needs hero companies, just like it always did. US news channels obsess over Google's share price as a measure of national success, just as they once would have focused on General Motors. Like the newspaper entrepreneur William Randolph Hearst, Mark Zuckerberg and his media influence (for better or worse) have been mythologised on screen. Today, of course, technology means these titans move at warp speed: whereas Hearst was in his 70s by the time *Citizen Kane* was released, Zuckerberg was still in his 20s when *The Social Network* premiered.

Ours is a time that celebrates the new, right now. But in our enthusiasm for the latest innovations and start-ups, we often forget that many very modern businesses' successes stem from timeless values. That's partially a matter of how a company is perceived by people, but it's also very much about how it treats people. It's about remembering the little things as you race towards your grander goals.

Google is a case in point. When people visit one of the company's offices for the first time, they don't just speak about the futuristic wonders they've witnessed; they talk about the awesome cafeteria and how lucky those who work there are to have licence to raid it.

In a world where automated communication is effortless and cheap, we appreciate the personal touches. Modern movements such as slow food, the craft renaissance and the celebration of all things 'artisan and vintage' also bear witness to a craving for classic virtues to complement modern, on-demand virtual lives.

At a glance, digital might superficially seem the antithesis of that craft ethos. But done properly, it's the best modern means we have of embodying that ethos for the masses. If late 20th-century branding was based on consumer goods mass-produced to be outward signifiers of success and status, then its future is about digital services that not only extend and enhance the resilience of products but also change the rules of consumerism.

Today, it's more about what you share online, not own offline. It's much less about the device you carry but how you connect with others. An obvious example is in the way that, in the past, the book or newspaper you were reading was an unavoidably public status symbol. But now, when you're reading your iPad, nobody knows whether it's the *Financial Times*, *Finnegan's Wake*, or *Fifty Shades*.

This shift in how we attribute value to goods and services will continue and intensify. The appeal of innovative future products will be as much about their smart digital connections as their physical forms.

That's not to stay we'll suddenly stop appreciating craft or artisanship; more that we will see their values applied thoughtfully and holistically. As good entrepreneurs have known for centuries, it's not about making the sale, but, rather, about keeping the customer satisfied.

Old values and customs are important precisely because they've been road-tested in real human societies over decades, centuries or even longer. Today, the most interesting innovations are often the ones that use technology to reconnect with old goals in new ways.

Science Exchange, for example, is a service that enables people working in a laboratory to pool their resources instead of duplicating research and renting equipment others already own. You put the parts of the work you can't do in-house out to tender by other members, to the point where you could conduct experiments in anti-gravity on the International Space Station. So it's not only 'modern' in the sense that it's bringing great efficiencies and expanding access. It's also old-fashioned in that it embodies the founding principle of the discipline of science itself, namely a sworn devotion to expand knowledge and human enlightenment.

Yourmechanic.com does something similar for consumer-level science by allowing car owners to find mechanics who can fix their cars on their properties, on their terms. The site takes care of the payments, the references and the terms, then the mechanic and the driver just do the job. In offering verified work histories, impartial expert advice and a binding quote system for jobs, the site does all the things that people have always wished automotive repair chains would. In doing so, it makes the idea of service – too often an empty name for a cynical revenue stream – a meaningful value once again.

You don't have to own a car to benefit from this kind of new-old improvement. Silvercar, the airport car rental service newly established at Dallas Fort Worth Airport, uses digital technology to reassert the eternal values of simplicity and thoughtful curation in enhancing user experiences. As well as eschewing excessive charges for refuelling and other staple car rental complaints, the company's entire fleet is composed of a single (silver) model, an Audi A4 with all the trimmings, including Wi-Fi. The accompanying smartphone app is designed to prevent the queues, hidden charges and compromises that we'd previously had to endure but never accepted as reasonable or pleasurable.

Nest is a young company that places value on something that has been a priceless human preoccupation since the dawn of time: keeping warm. The new-age thermostat maker also puts a value on something that's a real concern in more and more people's lives: the price of fuel, both to the consumer and the environment. Its thermostat uses your Wi-Fi network to learn about and respond to your behaviour around the house and prevent wasted energy. It's the ancient value of caring, in action.

Everlane is a clothing company that cuts costs to improve value, just as so many great modern fashion businesses have (think of Mickey Drexler and his save-on-the-marketing-budget, feel-the-quality ethos at J.Crew). Its promise to its customers is that by cutting out the management and marketing tiers needed to operate at physical retail, it gives them clothes that ultimately work and look better for them at a better price. It feels like the future – and, not un-coincidentally, like the best of the past too. In the UK, until the 1950s, the average working man got all his shirts and clothes made to measure at his high-street tailor. That wasn't because he was rich; it was because that was the best, most convenient way to make his budget and his outfit work for him.

Opening up areas by offering better value in them is one of the eternal values of the entrepreneur. Old values intelligently applied through new technologies can democratise markets and extend access to experiences, goods and services. New businesses, with their lack of vested interests or reasons to fear risk, are often best positioned to get back in touch with those values. You let more people have the things lots of people have always wanted. That's not an ethos I will ever regard as out of date.

— First published in Fast Company *in April 2013 —*

An operating system for life

Put technology to work for people and you're already taking steps towards that inspirational aspiration

In an economy obsessed by innovation, we're always on the lookout for cool little start-ups, clever new ways technology is changing our culture and smart new software that comes out of nowhere to show us a better way of doing things. When you watch the evolution of popular digital culture – and observe which services people love and are loyal to, which they get infatuated and then bored with, which they ignore and which they actively resent – you get fascinating results.

The era of services accessed through mobile phones has shown us that people respond to tools configured around (to quote Apple) "solving life's little problems, one app at a time". With this resounding user-focused lesson in mind, maybe the next big thing for us is something a little grander. Perhaps we should strive towards a world where we can promise an operating system for life – not as an immediate practical aspiration but as an idea that new examples of digital products and services ultimately take us closer towards.

The *Oxford English Dictionary* says an operating system is: "A set of programs for organising the resources and activities of a computer". Today, people respond to and embrace software that in some way organises their resources (time and money) and activities (work and play). Even a smartphone game you play in the supermarket is organising your resources, in this case time, by giving you an activity, sparing you the feeling of watching time pass by.

This week, we launched Nike+ Kinect Training, where an ongoing exchange of fine-tuned data gives people an evolving, precise and truly personal training system, improving health and fitness. In September, California's governor Jerry Brown signed the bill that legalised autonomous vehicles – also known as self-driving cars. Doing so wasn't just about space-age headlines but a response to the findings of initial research by companies such as Google, which suggest computer-controlled drivers can be safer and more efficient than humans.

Luddites might see such developments as the machines taking over, but the rest of us should be able to embrace this example of technology making efficient use of our time and resources. Here's the proof: Nissan recently unveiled early developments from its own autonomous vehicle research program. One part of the technology uses sensors and cameras to understand the spatial terrain around the car and respond accordingly, so drivers can't mistakenly move into too-small spaces or bump into unseen objects, and they won't have to correct driving lines. The second key innovation is the replacement of all the mechanical components between the steering wheel and front wheels with electronics for a much quicker, more responsive and driver-aware experience.

Back in the early 60s, Marshall McLuhan wrote an essay called 'The Gadget Lover: Narcissus as Narcosis'. In it, he surveyed the new boom in consumer electronics in America over the previous decade and identified a new archetype: the gadget lover. McLuhan wasn't overly enthusiastic about this emerging obsession, seeing it as a way for consumers to offload the information overload and psychic stress of modern life. The gadget was a kind of cyborg extension of the individual that helped them cope by putting them into a kind of trance (narcosis). Though the gadget lover sang the praises of the latest gadget for its innovations, they actually, unwittingly, loved it because it reflected their own interests and personality back, like a mirror.

We often want help, because we like to do things more easily and quickly, to better manage our resources and activities. We invest ourselves and our personalities in our technology – that's when it becomes interesting and relevant. We like technology to help do more useful and fun things; to make boring things less painful; and to save us time, money and misery.

People have become accustomed to having hardware and software working for them, and the internet has made everybody accustomed to having their say and expecting solutions at speed. If we love gadgets and software, it's precisely because we know they reflect our lives. We're not the deluded slaves of new gadgets – we're their impatient masters. New technologies give us more knowledge and control than we are used to. If I go to a firm such as 23andMe and pay $299 (£185) to get my genes analysed, that's not because I want to outsource my identity to machines – it's because the information they give me from a saliva sample will help me learn all sorts of interesting things, from past ancestry to future health problems, that I couldn't have accessed before.

In September, think tank Demos issued a report on people's attitudes to sharing data in the digital world. 'The Data Dividend' was written on the assumption that, used properly, big data can help all of us – at home, in healthcare, in civic life and in science – but thanks to high-profile loss-es of confidential information, expensive IT projects gone wrong, perceived heavy-handedness and newsworthy errors in its past application, many peo-ple are exceptionally cautious about the risks involved and the likelihood of promised benefits materialising.

What organisations need to do, then, is be modular and reactive. Use the data now generated by people's choices and behaviours to keep refining and improving their systems and making them more responsive. This means com-bining data with small, speedy manoeuvres – combining clear, reassuring, deeply held principles with agility and enough leeway for an organisation's employees to use the real-time data available to improve the services they offer.

TheyWorkForYou.com is the address where you can cut through the promotional materials and see how your MP acted where it counted, at key parliamentary votes. In a digital era where 'service' is the key aspiration for anybody hoping to continue engaging with people, organisations should take that message to heart. It may be too late for the 2012 US presidential elec-tions, but it's surely a more sensible way to re-engage voters in the data-rich, increasingly transparent world we inhabit today. Put technology to work for people and you're already taking steps towards that inspirational near-future aspiration: creating an operating system for our lives.

— First published in The Guardian *in November 2012 —*

Radically simple designs always win

The best digital innovations are ones that are simple and easy to use and keep your audience in mind

One of the most successful iPad word-processing apps over the past couple of years is iA Writer, a simple tool that gets rid of all the options, font choices, distractions and corrections that come with more elaborate programs. It has won a lot of fans by doing one thing very simply. Its creator, Oliver Reichenstein, has likened it to a scalpel in a world of Swiss Army knives.

iA Writer is an example of how powerful simplicity and accessibility can be for creating commercially successful interfaces, applications or services. This is true even if you're a newbie up against the software world's leading heavyweights.

Encode accessibility into your approach from the beginning, and you can connect with people in ways that existing designs have missed.

The proof is everywhere. MySpace was undone by the ease of use, utility and streamlined look of Facebook. The busy menus and options of previous search engines like AltaVista quickly became history by the clear white space and staggeringly beautiful simplicity of the Google homepage.

Remember the complex payment plans for 32-volume printed editions of *Encyclopedia Britannica*? Or Encarta, the disc-based digital encyclopedia, which had a 16-year run from its debut in the early 1990s? Both were perceived as out of date before they reached audiences. The best place to find out more about them today is on the site that made their demise inevitable: Wikipedia.

Google Translate blossomed thanks to similar logic. In a world of slow, pricey professional translation, its automated and free service launched in beta form and made no claims to perfection, but its accessibility made up for early limitations. Vast numbers of people felt invited and empowered to use the service, and the many millions of words they contributed helped make it better and more accurate. Speech technology company Nuance made its free Dragon Dictation application even more accurate using the same model.

TED is another digital success story. It shows how giving people something enriching gets rewards as long as you aren't greedy or needlessly confusing and as long as you don't take the attention of your busy, easily distracted audience for granted. To attend in person or receive TED's more exclusive perks via membership is an expensive business, but you can watch an inspirational, jargon-free lecture in 15 minutes for free without having to look further than YouTube; that's the definition of accessible, radical and user-friendly knowledge-sharing.

In a digital context, accessibility brings exponential improvements because a big and broad range of users means you can refine, deepen and improve your algorithms and databases by learning directly from a vast range of real human interactions. The more people try your tools, the better you are able to make them work.

Even if you don't have big budgets, you can still harness and combine a wealth of newly available digital tools to make something easier to create scale. Take Hailo for example. Created by a group of cab drivers and entrepreneurs, Hailo uses location data and connected apps for drivers and customers to prevent drivers chugging around wasting fuel and pedestrians from getting stuck out at night. It has smaller commissions and no specialist tech beyond a phone app.

Improvements can also be made on what digital pioneers have already done. In a world where only diehards get around to actually printing their photos, the importance of Facebook has always been, in large part, as a virtual photo album, which family and friends can access in seconds. But when Instagram came along, it made this process – point, click, post-produce and share – radically easy and more accessible still, and it thrived because of it.

A defining feature of the smartphone-equipped world is that we almost always have the option to look elsewhere if somebody overcomplicates their offering or takes us for granted. That's why it's increasingly rare for difficult-to-navigate shopping experiences to survive. We might struggle on despite the bad design if the commodity is desirable or exclusive, but we'll also make sure we tell the world what we think about it – the miseries of the London 2012 Olympic ticketing site are a case in point.

We can pinpoint the demise of so many companies to the moment they became over-busy and fussy to navigate. Typically, there are two ways in which this happens.

In the first case, the designers, coders and editorial people are so obsessed with what they make that they forget the rest of us have to use it too. They can't get back into the mindset of the audience, so they lose sight of where the mass appeal and effectiveness of their service lies. A redesign that forces people to elaborately customise, rather than just continue to utilise a service, can be enough to put swathes of them off using it at all.

The second problem is when the tools, services, communications or data-mining demands make a successful service an unsuccessful one by ruining whatever it was that made your game, site, app or whatever so pleasurable in the first place.

'The interface determines the interaction' is one of those digital truths to keep in mind. But striving for accessibility is nothing to do with dumbing down; rather, it is about having the discipline to intercept and reject snobbery, pretension or arrogance. The art of accessibility is about working out how to make what you do well available to the greatest number of people without compromising its essence.

— *First published in* The Guardian *in August 2012* —

The best
leaders don't
raise their
voices.

They raise
standards.

Share of
market

STEMS FROM

share
of mind.

DON'T CONFUSE HUMILITY

WITH WEAKNESS

Good work

is about the vision to question the **status quo,** to challenge the confines of convention by daring to be an agent of change

that's at the
vanguard,
not the
old guard.

DISCIPLINE IS THE ENGINE THAT GETS GOALS

TO GLORY

Words can be _enchanting_, but there's no substitute for **truthful action**.

An audience only remembers the weight of your words, not how often you speak.

Today's triumphs can
quickly become tomorrow's
traditions. Yet, ideas are the
messengers of potential.

They are the seeds of hope that
drive out the darkness and the
antidote to despair. Ideas are
the all-emcompassing force that
holds the world together.

It is within ideas that we
all find one another.

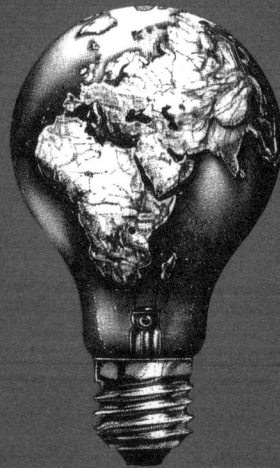

It's stories that change

the world, not:

- bullet points

- or indeed bullets.

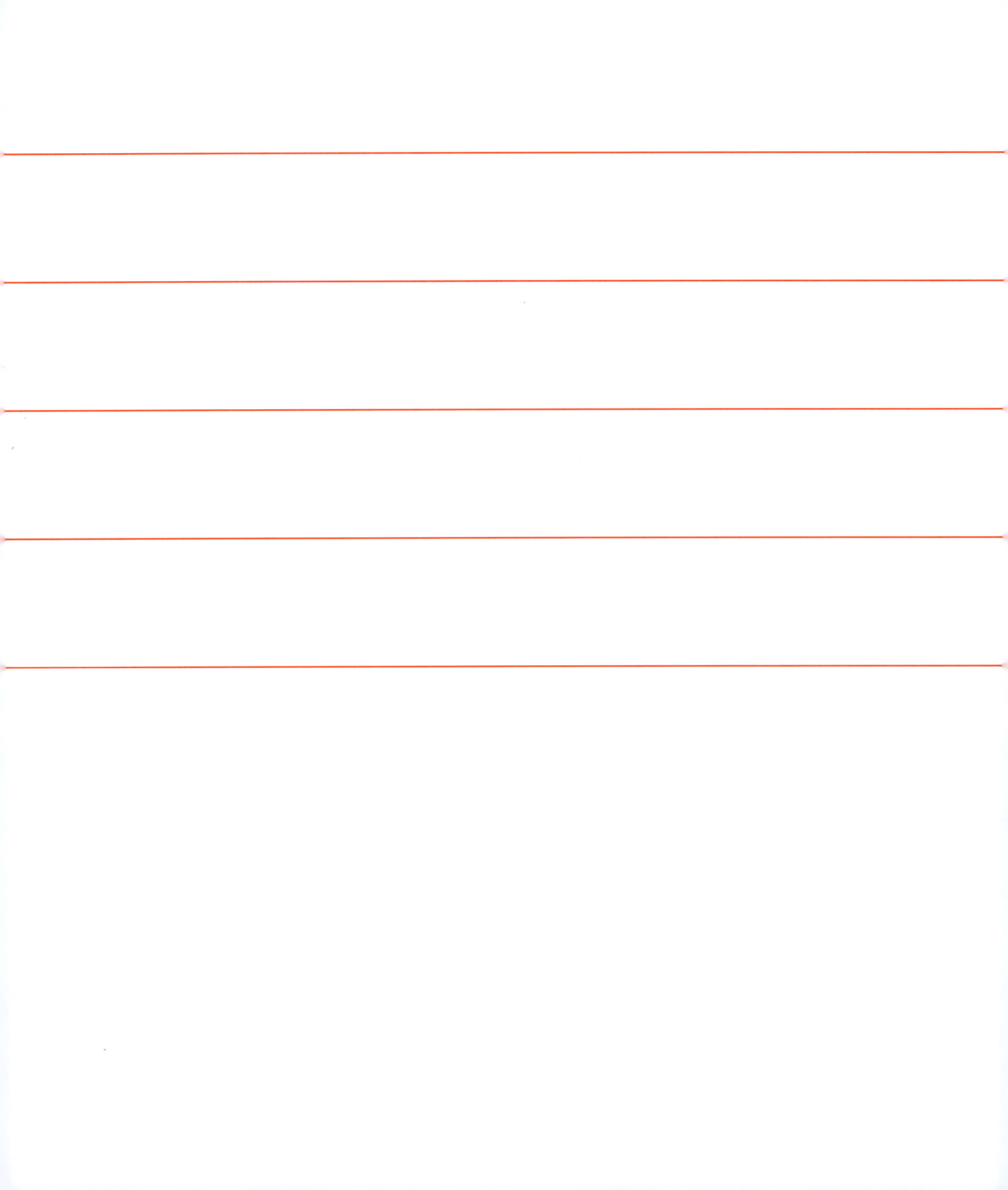

A new destination
may take time,
but a new
direction starts
with a single turn.

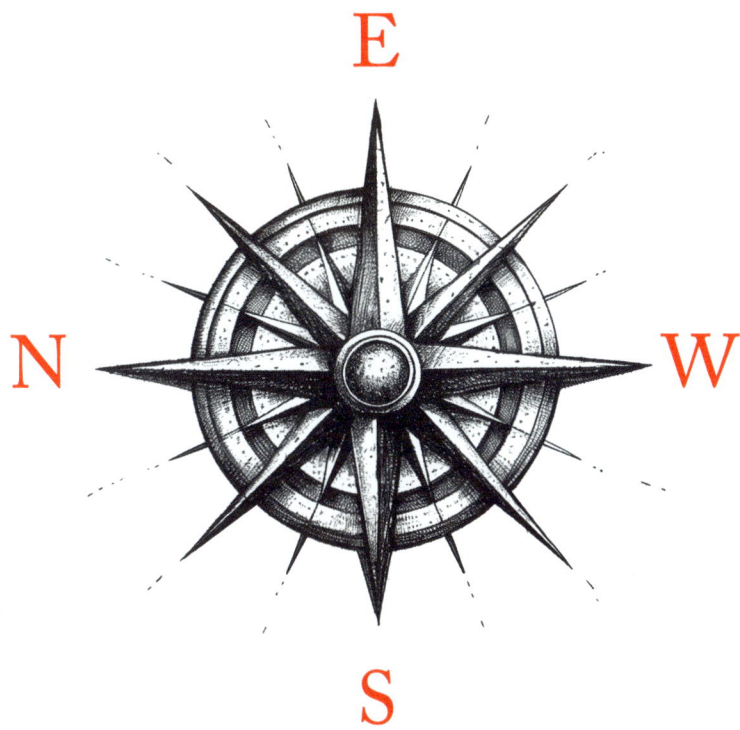

Dispatches

Emails 2000–2024

What follows is a chronological sequence of excerpts from internal emails sent to colleagues at AKQA – sometimes to the entire company, other times to a particular team. Collected and reprinted this way, it's also the story of the past quarter-century of working life at AKQA. These pages record key moments in our journey and, in so doing, document the way the business world at large went digital over the three decades since our founding. They also track the ways our defining objective of exploring new terrain saw us expand from the online realm and back into working with some of my first loves: physical design, architecture and the wider environment. Some messages are included because they're snapshots of long-gone technologies and terms of engagement; others, because they express ideas that feel just as relevant today.

2001 HERE WE COME   DECEMBER 2000

Those of you who were here in 1999 will know that 2000 was always going to be a challenging year to meet the demanding and increasingly complex needs of our clients. We met that challenge, and as we end the year in a strong position, it's worth reflecting on some of the things that made a difference while also looking towards 2001 and the new challenges it will bring.

Although we had successes in 2000, we also had some setbacks. At times, I felt that as a company we were being complacent. We weren't always on the ball or true to our values, and that resulted in client and employee disappointments.

Despite the changes in 2001, we will always be a company driven by certain key philosophies.

First and foremost, AKQA is dedicated to innovation and the passion to create a great product for our clients. Whether it's the launch of an e-shop on the web or the development of a new online advertising campaign, we make every effort to take our client's customer to where they want to go before they realise that they want to go there. Clients hire AKQA because we understand that customers rule. Customers make all the important decisions.

If the client's customer isn't buying, then our clients have problems and we have problems. When our clients can see that we're adding value and helping them to be more successful is when they have healthy relationships with their customers, and we have healthy relationships with our clients.

GREAT IDEAS AND DEPTH   OCTOBER 2001

I've recently had the chance to spend some time with AKQA clients.

What fascinated and worried me in equal measure was the disconnect between what the client wants ('sell more of my products', 'build my brand', 'make me look good') and what actually gets briefed in/done.

Think about how many projects you have been involved in that have helped our clients to become measurably more successful. You can always tell if an idea is a good one because, if it is, the client's customer flocks to it. If the client's customer doesn't go to it in droves, the idea and its execution sucks.

More often than not, this industry simply produces brochures with buttons: identikit websites that don't offer what consumers crave or the benefits that clients need.

Agencies bore their clients with charts and processes, rather than brilliant ideas, well executed. Clients crave brilliant ideas because ideas are fuel.

A lot of the work out there is just plain boring. It doesn't get noticed, and if you're a brand, the worst thing that can happen to you is not getting noticed.

AKQA's premise is simple: We think of ideas that help our clients to succeed. It doesn't matter who the client is or what business they are in, the more creative the idea, the more chance it has of being successful.

IT WOULD BE OK IF IT WASN'T FOR THE CLIENTS... APRIL 2002

I don't think you can be good in this business unless you love what you do and actually want to help clients through producing brilliant work. It's true of every discipline, whether you work in technology, creative or accounts.

Admittedly, this is asking for a lot of commitment. But we do work for the best brands, and we do strive to be the best ourselves.

So anyone who thinks that we are in servitude or conflict with clients is a fool. And anyone who is getting in the way of helping to develop a partnership with clients should find a new career.

WORKING AS A TEAM AUGUST 2002

Everything is going digital, and the fact that we are the bridge that takes our clients from analogue to digital puts us in a great position – a position that we would be foolish to relinquish.

I don't think that we can make progress without having respect for one another and without working better as a team. All our victories and all our successes have been achieved when we have worked together. All our failures come when we are selfish.

I don't think you get teamwork from expensive corporate team-building events, or through group hugs, or even through sending emails. I don't think you get teamwork through pursuing individual glory. I know that the only way we can work better is when we have respect for one another, when we share and benefit from one another's knowledge and talent, when we make sacrifices, when we put aside power struggles and focus on individual accomplishment so that it benefits the team.

Teamwork is the fuel that has allowed us to achieve the impossible. Team is and always will be the critical ingredient in achieving success for our clients and ourselves.

It's a reality of life that people are competitive, but we must compete not with one another but with those companies that do better work or have better ideas than we do.

Most advertising is lacking in four critical ways that, if remedied, would make it more engaging to web and online:

• Lack of ideas
If an idea is good, then almost any kind of execution will make it work, but you can never make a bad idea work using even the best execution. That's why it's always important to have a strong idea and theme for all the work we produce. Sometimes that theme is inspired through integrated marketing campaigns, and other times it needs to be invented, but there always needs to be an idea – a platform for the creativity.

• Absence of interactivity
It's always fascinating to me that, although digital media offers a vast number of benefits over traditional media, people do not use this interactivity to benefit the work they are developing. Ideas that do not have any interactivity or don't provide a benefit over traditional media usually fail.

• Lack of simplicity
Less is indeed more. The more you take out, the more effective it will usually be. For some reason, the web has too many overly elaborate, complex ideas that could be much simpler. People should not cram many ideas into activity and instead should adopt fewer ideas but execute those brilliantly, adding depth and focus to them. The same is true for copy. Copy should be edited so that it uses fewer words.

• Not visually compelling enough
Not all activity is visually compelling or exciting. And if it is not visually compelling, then it's boring, and boring work does not engage customers. The world of digital entertainment is visually rich because of amazing special effects in feature films and video games. Consumers expect the same from the web, but it is not being delivered.

Every so often something happens in AKQA's history that I describe as a 'defining moment'.

Sometimes that moment is a great idea or the way we approach a pitch or a strategy presentation. Sometimes it's the successful completion of a project that seemed more challenging than anything before it. Other times it's when a team or an individual makes a big difference to the company.

Defining moments are special because they make the ordinary, extraordinary. They turn something that could have quite easily been an everyday occurrence into something that completely changes the way that we think about our work. Defining moments move the company forward.

As one of the youngest companies in the communications and technology industry, I've never counted the years we have been in business as a measure of our success because I prefer to count AKQA's progress in terms of the number of defining moments.

Having had the opportunity over the past few days to spend time with our clients, I wanted to share with you three tips that I believe will be useful for your careers.

If we implement these consistently, then I truly believe that our relationships with clients will grow stronger, our quality control and attention to detail will be better and the standard of our work will be exceptional:

1. Make your client look good
Through the work we do, we have the ability to make our clients heroes. We can create work that is a success story and helps to move our client companies forward while inspiring other people in their organisation and industry. In everything we do, we should be focussed on ensuring that all the work we do enhances our client's brand and reputation. We should not be afraid of innovation and creative solutions while at the same time only making promises that we can keep.

2. Treat the client's business as your own
When you treat a client's business like your own, you show a passion, interest and dedication that cannot go unnoticed. You also understand what the client's competitors are doing, you understand the challenges that the client's business faces and you understand the client's customer. This knowledge

equips you to provide a better solution and also seek opportunities to help the client's business. Treating the client's business like your own should mean that you act with consistency, honesty and integrity in all your dealings. You should want to make your client's business the leader in their sector.

3. Think about the client's customer

If the work that we do does not have a positive impact on the client's customer, then there's pretty much no point doing it. We should be inspiring, motivating and delighting our client's customer. Creativity, simplicity, customer insight and common sense helps us to do this.

QUALITY CONTROL

Quality control is not two people sat at their desks checking code or one person checking copy.

Quality control is everyone's responsibility to ensure that the work we produce functions as its purpose dictates. It means we follow process, and following process means that everything is tested. It means that we check and double-check everything before putting it live or sending anything to a client. It means that we acutely understand the duty of care we owe to our client's and their customers.

It means that we check again once the work is live, and we keep checking to make sure everything works.

Because that's what we get paid to do.

THANK YOU

Yesterday, I was asked by a client to tell them why we are different from the others? Why has AKQA been successful?

I explained that our people have gratitude. We are grateful to be a part of this company. We are grateful to work with great clients who want us to produce great work.

I went on to explain that we built AKQA around a worthy purpose that continues to motivate us, and I hope always will.

Ours is not an obsession with growth. We are not interested in industry league tables. All we want to do is innovate and produce inspirational work that gets our clients results – we want to deliver. We want to do the right thing. This doesn't mean we don't want to grow. We do – growth provides new opportunities, but our commitment to our values must always be ahead of growth.

GREAT IDEAS ARE BOUGHT. THEY DON'T HAVE TO BE SOLD. APRIL 2004

When it comes to our work, there are two questions for me that are more important than anything else:

"Where's the innovation?" – "what are the results?"

And there is one message that resonates more so today than it has ever done: great ideas are bought; they don't have to be sold.

What this means is that when a client can see a great idea, they buy it.

They buy it because it's good for their business. It's good for their customer and it's good for their career.

If we're to build the client's business. If we're to become our client's trusted adviser. If we're to get continued acclaim for our work. If we're to expand our connection with our clients at home and globally – and I want us to do all of this – then the only currency we have is our ability to innovate.

VALUING OUR VALUES AUGUST 2004

On Saturday night, I was lucky enough to have dinner with the co-author of the bestselling business book in history.

The book he wrote has become legendary. It defined the era. And because he wrote it, he is considered a legend too. So while spending five minutes in his company would have been good, to have had three courses worth of conversation was an absolute privilege.

The timing of the dinner was perfect as right now I'm feeling more excited about AKQA than ever. The business is growing; we've got the best people and are attracting more; we have a great client list; and we're delivering quality work. All good. But good is never really good enough.

So I used the opportunity to seek counsel. I asked him what makes good companies great? He told me that all great companies have a set of values that everyone upholds in everything the company does. I then asked him what makes a good company turn into a bad one? He told me that when good companies betray their values, they turn bad.

So I learned two things that night:

First, a reaffirmation of everything that AKQA stands for. It reminded me that our values of Innovation, Service, Quality and Thought are more important as we grow than they have ever been.

And second, I learned that nothing is impossible. If a university dropout can have dinner with the author of the bestselling business book in history, then why can't AKQA become the best company in our industry? Certainly that's the goal.

Last week I sent an email about operational excellence. This is the definition for me:

- Providing all staff with fair reward and recognition for their contribution, hard work and loyalty
- Not taking anything for granted
- Ensuring that all staff work in a good environment
- Avoiding the use of freelancers and instead investing in our own talent and growing it
- Hiring someone only when there is space to hire them and a good manager to provide mentoring
- Delighting clients through great ideas which in turn create great results
- Being well-organised so that the company can get information at the touch of a button
- Ensuring that our systems provide us with information because people use the systems
- Taking on new business pitches only when we can actually deliver the work and the pitch without compromise
- Investing in our four core pillars of Strategy, Creative, Technology and Management
- Making time for creativity, ideas and growing our minds instead of just growing the business
- Breaking the rules when the best thing to do is break the rules

Of course, there is more. But these are some of the key priorities for AKQA London to create a quality business that's strong and wise for the long term. As Tom [Bedecarré, AKQA chairman] said, "in a world of consolidation, AKQA should be the consolidator of talent."

We need to work together to ensure that we achieve these goals because when we do, we will create a better business, and that's got to be good for everyone.

I want AKQA to be a fun, creative place to work because it's the right thing to do.

Ten years ago, AKQA predicted that the digital revolution would be the most significant catalyst for change that the media world had experienced. That prediction has come true. Ten years ago AKQA was founded for one reason: to bring our clients success through the innovative application of new technologies. This continues to be our mission today. Ten years ago, AKQA had different competition to the competition we have today and that competition continues to change and intensify.

Our clients have always had high expectations and it is an honour to serve them. We're fortunate that there are many more clients who want to work with AKQA, and because the digital revolution is just starting, the opportunities for this company are limitless.

For me, AKQA is about a purity of purpose. We exist to think of ideas that will bring success to our clients. It's really that simple. When we do this, we grow our relationships. When we don't, our relationships inevitably contract.

I'd like to take this opportunity to thank all the people in the company who keep their promises, who are passionate about delivering success for their clients and who know it is their responsibility to champion groundbreaking work. These are the future of AKQA.

ADVERTISING AGE NAMES AKQA ON ITS A-LIST   JANUARY 2008

I'm delighted to let you know that this morning *Advertising Age* magazine has named AKQA one of its A-List.

This is a very special honour, considering that from the thousands of agencies around the world to choose from, only 10 made it, and AKQA is one of them. Our chairman, Tom Bedecarré, is featured on the front cover.

"They're on the cutting edge, defying classification, willing to experiment and retaining top talent," said *Advertising Age*, adding, "take a long look at AKQA, an agency that's very quietly turning itself into a full-service marketing partner that just happens to have digital roots. AKQA has long been among the best when it comes to designing websites and interactive ad programmes; now it's branching out to shape customer experience in a bigger way."

When you consider that AKQA has won two Agency of the Year awards this year alone and *Marketing* magazine called out AKQA as a creative leader in the UK, describing us as moving into a league of its own, it's a very special and unique way to start to the year.

We now have about 700 employees around the world, making us I think the largest independent agency network, and judging from the incredible international recognition our agency is getting, one of the most respected and talked about too.

AKQA NAMED ONE OF THE WORLD'S MOST
INNOVATIVE COMPANIES

Last October, *Fast Company* magazine set out to identify the world's most innovative companies. The magazine asked reporters around the globe to gather data and interview experts and business leaders in every industry to get nominations. The final 50 were selected from a list of 300 finalist companies. We are honoured that AKQA is in that 'Fast 50'.

We sincerely believe that questioning the status quo, refusing to follow the conventional path, finding the better way to do things, making integrity and great work our priority and seeking long-term partnership with our team and clients are the reasons.

When we launched AKQA internationally seven years ago, we wanted it to be a new kind of agency – an agency with innovation at its core and one that would help its clients lead in the digital age. It's one thing to believe that everything we do should be about innovation, but it's another to get recognition for it. When that recognition also names the companies we love and admire the most – Nike, Nokia, Apple, Google and Facebook – it means so much more. And when the write-up about AKQA compares us to Pixar and mentions our world-class creative and technology expertise working in harmony, it truly is an honour.

Today, it's exciting that in the process of building great brands AKQA has also become a respected international brand.

Other awards and honours AKQA received in 2008 included a New York Times article that credited the agency and its work with Apple, in creating apps for Gap and Target and in its work with NikeLab; at the British Interactive Multimedia Association's awards, AKQA won eight awards, including Agency of the Year (a second successive win) and the Grand Prix.

We believe in creating a culture where our team is motivated to create the best work of their careers. This means a meritocracy that encourages ideas and contributions from every area of the company. It rewards determination, innovation and the discipline to deliver.

We believe in growth because that's when progress occurs. Growth means new clients. Expanding existing relationships. It means taking care of business at home while starting adventures in new markets.

We believe in profit because it gives us the freedom to make the right decisions that allow us to grow. It also means that we have the choice to work with clients that we believe in.

We believe in the transformative power of good ideas. These may start as embryos but when nurtured can become giants. It means lots of small ideas executed well are just as powerful as a big idea.

We believe in the power of the virtuous circle – that if we do good, then good things will happen. It means taking responsibility to create work that moves the needle for our clients and delights their audiences.

We put soul and humanity into our work and culture so that we don't take for granted what we have or where we aspire to go next. It means we don't take ourselves too seriously that we might forget that we're lucky to do something we love with people we respect.

Twenty-twelve was a busy year for the company. AKQA saw success with its Future Lions awards for promising young talent after teething troubles on its debut the year before. AKQA Insight, a knowledge-sharing platform, launched. The company won a number of honours, including multiple Agency of the Year awards. With co-author Stefan Olander, then of Nike, Ajaz Ahmed published the bestseller Velocity, *a guide to doing business in a world gone digital.*

NICE WAY TO START THE WEEK   SEPTEMBER 2013

Hi, everyone,

Below are a few sentences from an email our client sent to Sir Martin Sorrell the other day. (For client confidentiality, the brand name has been removed.) Our aspiration is to create influential work that people love and get this kind of feedback from every client we work with:

"Dear Sir Martin,

As you may be aware we recently engaged your agency AKQA as our partner to assist on the journey of repositioning our brand and to enable our digital transformation. In little more than five weeks, the team at AKQA have exceeded all expectations and have been an utter to joy to work with. AKQA's professionalism, obsession with the finest details (so important for a luxury brand), have been awe inspiring and all this without losing sight of our launch objective. The icing on the cake came today when my CEO presented the work to our board members who gave the work a standing ovation…[the launch event] will provide an informal setting for me to introduce you to our CEO so that he can thank you personally for the support from AKQA."

THE STORY OF A 14-YEAR LOVE AFFAIR   JULY 2013

Team,

This year we celebrate the 14th year of AKQA's partnership with Nike.

To mark this moment, I'm reflecting a little on the past and more so on the present.

Looking back, I recently unearthed a beautiful magazine that AKQA produced when we celebrated our fifth birthday.

Nike designed the back cover of the magazine. Featuring an athlete, arms victorious in the air, its headline reads:

"If something is going to live with you forever, why is it called a moment?"

That's the way I will always feel about Nike.

Looking ahead, it's worth remembering that some of our best work has not been in response to a briefing.

We found an occasion, hit on an insight, revealed a problem that needs fixing or invented an opportunity that's just too good to miss.

We gave an artist the perfect canvas; we put a technology to good use; we unleashed genius.

Don't wait for a set of instructions.

Just do it.

There is no finish line.

AKQA VALUES AND PURPOSE

We exist to create the future with our clients.

We do this through the imaginative application of art and science to create beautiful ideas that move the world.

We invent labours of love, the work that captivates people in unexpected ways.

That's why we say the most powerful force in the universe isn't technology. It's imagination.

Innovation, Service, Quality and Thought are our foundations.

And we work with people who share these values.

We believe in the virtuous cycle:

Good intentions + Good work = Great outcomes

We chase perfection.

And are in conflict with mediocrity.

We democratise what's for the few and make it accessible to many.

We do this with the belief that the simple will always displace the complex.

Through artistry and craftsmanship, we seek inner satisfaction, rather than outer recognition.

We take a brief this _ small

And make it an opportunity this _____ big

But we are only as good as our next idea.

And we are always thinking, "What's next?"

We are a work in progress.

The future inspires us, we work to inspire.

Demand for our work is the strongest it's ever been. And it's true that sometimes, when creating a labour of love, we all put in long hours and sometimes we all feel burdened by deadlines; but the exhilaration will hopefully always outweigh the exhaustion.

We create something, so there is satisfaction. We do it as a team, so there is friendship, and we do something useful and inspiring, so there is a sense of purpose.

Often when companies talk about growth, they are talking about size. But our focus is growth of excellence across everything we do.

Passion, conscientiousness, adaptability, loyalty and integrity are integral qualities that we look for in the people we hire. We recognise that AKQA's continued progression and innovation for clients rests on our ability to attract, develop and retain the finest talent.

Right now we are on the search for fantastic people to join our team. We put particular emphasis on the following characteristics:

Adventurousness
Imagination
Passion
Leadership
Flexibility
Conscientiousness

On Monday night I received a letter from one of our clients that said, "You've stood with us on the frontier of our ambition and walked alongside us…Your presence is critical because we're still in a relationship business. People matter. Time together matters. Relationships matter."

Yesterday I got a message that said, "Your team is beyond excellent". This from a client that believed in our youth and our hunger over 15 years ago, gave us a long shot at proving they made the right decision and remains proud to see our team raise the bar to this day.

We might have been naive back then, but we did realise one thing: the only way of keeping this – and any other client – is demonstrating the same level of hunger, drive and determination every single day.

The past five years have been an extraordinary opportunity for us to focus on what we're good at and learn where we can be better.

Five years ago we had 1,160 employees. Today, we are closer to 2,000. Five years ago we had significantly fewer employee shareholders, with less value, than we do today. Five years ago we didn't have studios in Atlanta, Auckland, Gothenburg, Melbourne, Paris, Portland, São Paulo, Sydney, Tokyo or Venice. Today we do.

In 2018, AKQA's range of skills and services was dramatically expanded when interior design practice Universal Design Studio and industrial design consultancy MAP joined the company. Another development was AKQA Framework, a blueprint for better performance combining principles and metrics. In 2019, the company once again scored big at the advertising industry's annual showcase in Cannes.

In challenging times – when barriers go up, and there is a global lockdown – self-preservation often becomes a primary focus.

While social isolation is prevention, now should be a time of unity, connection and togetherness.

We have the tools, resources and determination to do this and get through this.

Withstanding challenges with dignity starts with service: ensuring all are respected and being served in their time of need.

Where there is darkness be the candle that lights the way. Let people know they are not alone.

I am proud of our team, who I know are making sacrifices to serve the needs of loved ones, colleagues and community with patience, faith and strength.

If I can be of service and support to you, please let me know.

In 2021, branding and design agency Made Thought joined AKQA. Together with MAP and Universal Design Studio, it's part of a company-wide project to establish a new set of design principles and practices for brands – 'The New Standard'.

LOVE WIPES OUT FEAR
AKQA BLOOM SPRINGS INTO ACTION   MARCH 2022

Every entrepreneurial journey starts with leaping into the unknown with willingness.

Launching AKQA Bloom today alongside each of you is about being active participants in our love of this world, our love of life, our appreciation for all life and our reverence for the life-support systems we depend on.

We have always aimed to look beyond. To galvanise and harness the ideas of our time. The idea of launching AKQA Bloom does not feel like an act of rebellion, or dutiful or worthy, but a true response at a moment where we collectively face overwhelming ecological and social crises.

Human activities are causing the biosphere to deteriorate at an alarming rate, destroying climate viability for future generations. Global inequity, injustice, inequality and wealth disparity are accelerating. Two years of the pandemic have had a widespread ruinous impact, exacerbating social isolation, grief, anger and related trauma. We now live in the shadow of war and harrowing refugee tragedies fuelled by the insanity of conflict for diminishing natural resources in a world of possible abundance. But of all the dangers, perhaps indifference, passivity, suspicion and cynicism are the most significant.

These challenges of planetary anguish stimulate a different way of living, working, contributing and boldly reimagining towards something more healthy, hopeful, peaceful and sustainable. By launching AKQA Bloom, we are being intentional about playing our part in the process of renewal, reconciliation and healing. We are reclaiming a vision of hope in our hearts and a destination of interconnectedness to head for. We will grow from learning and elevate this into fearless ideas in harmony with all forms of life.

Information alone is not enough to alter patterns of behaviour. We have the resources, the ingenuity, the agency – and now the agency – to help transform despair and apathy into unity and rage and sorrow into courage for constructive, collaborative action.

We are launching AKQA Bloom to be more connected to our souls. We sow these seeds to better feel the pulse of our planet as a continual source of renewal. We plant these roots to gain new energies and new perspectives out of a profound sense of belonging as well as to show our participation in and our gratitude for this precious earth in the sincere belief that difficulties are not inevitable, challenges are not insurmountable and creative expression infused with meaning will help confront the obstacles. We have the opportunity to co-author a chapter, giving ourselves to a larger story of remedy and recovery that we can engage in together.

The days when advertising only existed to sell something are now long behind us. No brand can ignore the call, the responsibility and the obligation to be stewards of less consumption and more compassion.

Planet Earth is our client. It's time to Bloom.

IN A WORLD OF ONE-HIT WONDERS, CREATE THE WINNERS   JULY 2022

Dear Team,

Question: who gets turned to when…

Nike wanted to honour the story of its first 50 years, and look even further into the future?

Netflix, the world's most popular storyteller, needed to tell its tale?

Jio wanted to connect every heart in India?

H&M wanted to transform old clothes into new?

The new Elizabeth Line needed a lasting interior that would move millions for decades ahead?

The world wanted to thank Queen Elizabeth for her exceptional seven-decade reign?

The creator of Kingsman, Kick-Ass and Rocketman needed an identity for himself?

The real Rocketman wanted to reach the world in the middle of a global lockdown?

Space X went exploring to discover a new Mission Badge for its rockets?

Delta wanted every passenger to land a first-class experience?

IBM needed a crew to design its Quantum computer?

Google wanted to research devices that respect your needs without demanding your attention?

Sky wanted to design a new TV and ensure it got the attention of the nation?

Tennis Australia wanted to provide a different perspective for people with visual impairments?

The answer is you.

TOMORROW'S TRIUMPHS START WITH TODAY'S CREATIVITY   APRIL 2023

Dear Team,

AKQA is a place for visionaries, makers, pioneers and innovators.

We shine when we're designing, producing and problem-solving.

For us, practical execution transcends academic prowess.

We excel by creating the future, not archiving or preserving the past.

We recognise the immense privilege of having 19,590 individuals apply for a career at AKQA in just the past three months.

That's nearly 20,000 people inspired by the contribution we can make as a team.

We owe it to every applicant, our clients, audiences and one another to ensure professionalism and pride in everything we produce.

We are responsible for cultivating the culture and commercial acumen necessary to champion adaptability, responsiveness, resilience and financial stability for the long term.

The more work we make, the more we innovate.

The more we innovate, the more we make.

REFLECTING ON 30 YEARS OF INVENTIVE SPIRIT   SEPTEMBER 2024

I founded AKQA this week 30 years ago, and it has been my chief endeavour ever since.

In the time that has elapsed, AKQA has been honoured with 81 Agency of the Year wins; 11 Most Loved Workplace certifications; and many more awards, including 22 Cannes Lions and 25 D&AD distinctions this year.

Today's triumphs can quickly become tomorrow's traditions. Yet you never feel like you've done enough because the care this vocation asks of you – and which you want to give – is limitless.

I hope you agree that AKQA has always protected dreams, vision and values and aimed to create the labours of love, the sachets of delight and the pockets of excitement – the kind of work that rivets people in unexpected ways.

Ideas are the messengers of potential. They are the seeds of hope that drive out the darkness and the antidote to despair.

Ideas are the all-encompassing force that holds the world together.

It is within ideas that we all find one another.

ONE LAST THING   OCTOBER 2024

Dear Team,

I wrote to you a few weeks ago to celebrate our 30th year. Today, I am writing to let you know that I have resigned from AKQA.

Though my time at AKQA has ended, the work goes on, the ambition still burns, the desire to do better never leaves us and the dream shall never die.

Serving AKQA's team, clients and values for the past 30 years has been the greatest honour of my life. Founding AKQA at a young age was the start of an incredible journey, and if destiny allows, I look forward to another 30 years of meaningful work and making a difference.

Our path has always been guided by a bright light of goodness, illuminating the way ahead. You now carry the torch forward, pushing the boundaries of what's possible.

From the start, AKQA was more of an all-consuming calling than a company. My connection to AKQA has been my purpose, passion and devotion. It's been my whole adult life, an idea woven into every fibre of my being. Today, AKQA represents a living extension of our ethos, born from vision and nurtured with commitment and sacrifice.

In its infancy, AKQA took its first steps, stumbled and rose again. The triumphs were exhilarating, the defeats humbling, and both were integral to our journey. As I step aside, I have immense gratitude for all the lives that enhanced mine and the lessons we've taught each other along the way. I'm also eternally proud that our work has influenced countless people, improved many organisations and contributed positively to the world.

AKQA is internationally respected for its pioneering perspective, which proves that courage, curiosity and perseverance can overcome the toughest odds. One of the reasons I believe in serendipity is that the story of AKQA is one where the odds were always stacked against us, but somehow we made it from the basement to the boardrooms of the world's most inspirational brands.

The dotcom crash, the global financial crisis, the pandemic and the recent downturn have all tested our fortitude. But instead of retreating, we turned obstacles into opportunities. The challenging moments didn't break us – they made us stronger, more determined and more united. It has been in times of greatest uncertainty that our team has found its greatest strength.

Thank you for allowing me to be part of something truly special. Thank you for making AKQA a place where ideas come to life, where ingenuity knows no limits and where the future is always within reach. Thank you for your unwavering faith in the power of possibility and for the shared belief that there were no boundaries to what we could achieve.

As I move on from my responsibilities at AKQA, it's impossible for me to put into words my feelings about the lasting legacy we've created.

AKQA is your company, and its enduring values of Innovation, Service, Quality, and Thought are not just words – they are the foundation upon which we've built everything. They are what have set us apart and will continue to do so in the years to come. They are what will propel AKQA into tomorrow, ensuring that its work continues to inspire enriching progress.

My hope for AKQA is that your drive and determination will fuel the spirit of everything we have worked for. Though I will not be here day-to-day, my love for AKQA will remain constant.

Heartache, caused by the separation from something you love and helped bring into the world, can rob us of the ability to marvel at the wonders around us and steal the joy of seeing the beauty in this life. But I am not burdened by grief. This moment feels more like a rebirth, a door opening to something new.

There was undoubtedly a time when I needed AKQA more than it needed me. Today, I am blessed with two cheeky rascals, Aaron and Isaac, who have transformed my life in the most unexpected and wonderful ways. But I will always think of AKQA as my first child – one we all raised together. (The K in AKQA stands for Khowaj, my father's name; my middle name; and, serendipitously, my maternal grandfather's name too. *Khowaj* means 'spiritual guide and wisdom'.)

I've only ever written two farewell messages. The first was when I was 16 years old and worked part-time for the world's third-most valuable software company. My parting note ended with the realisation that, "Nothing in life worth having comes easy."

Over my three decades with AKQA, I've only become more certain that some simple, timeless truths are even more important. As I sign off today, it feels more appropriate than ever to say that the most powerful force in the universe isn't technology or imagination. It's love.

You can reach me at my new email: ajaz@ajaz.org

Don't forget to dream,

Ajaz

Entrepreneurship is
Another Word for Love
and Love isn't Playing it Safe

No one starts a venture
to hide from the wind
or to shelter from the rain.

Not just to weather the storms
but to sail straight into them.

Not to move with the tide
But turn the current.

Love runs wild on imagination.
It's the only capital that never runs dry
and we've got plenty to invest.

No high-rise schemers will dictate our dreams
or cage our freedom.

We won't sell our souls
to the gatekeepers of monotony.

We will have each other
hands making what our hearts believe in.

A time for new dreams is here.